SPIRITUAL FORMATION

SPIRITUAL FORMATION

Ever Forming, Never Formed

Peter K. Nelson

Biblica Publishing
We welcome your questions and comments.

USA   1820 Jet Stream Drive, Colorado Springs, CO 80921

Spiritual Formation
ISBN-13: 978-1-93406-882-3

A catalog record for this book is available through the Library of Congress.

Printed in the United States of America

Contents

In memory of my grandfather
Rev. Anton E. Sjolund (1892–1951)
Pastor, evangelist, student of God's Word
Godly guide on the way of spiritual formation

ACKNOWLEDGEMENTS

Over the last decade, in my own faith journey with Christ and while serving as a pastor and Bible professor, this book has been gradually taking shape in my mind. And along the way there have been many people who've provided me with vital input and support.

I presented seminar papers at the 2004 and 2005 Evangelical Theological Society annual meetings on themes related to this book. The feedback of colleagues, including those in the Spiritual Formation / Sanctification Section, was of great help in refining my thoughts about the interplay of growth in godliness and the ongoing battle against sin.

While teaching at Wheaton College there were numerous occasions to share my thoughts on "ever forming, never formed" with colleagues and students. In the laboratory of dialogue I was helped to ask new questions and probe God's Word deeply regarding spiritual formation. In particular, I'm grateful for the input of Jim Wilhoit, Scott Hafemann, Doug Moo, Sam Storms, and Gary Burge.

My church family (Goshen Baptist Church in West Chester, Pennsylvania) has been a center of joyful camaraderie for me as we've sought the Lord together and as I've carried on with this writing project. I thank the Lord for their partnership in the gospel. In 2007 I preached a sermon series called "Under Construction," focusing on the key Scriptures that would be foundational for this book. I'm grateful for the stimulating conversations and constructive feedback I received in connection with that series. Further, I thank the Lord for the prayer support from the small group at Goshen in which my wife and I have been involved.

Numerous friends and ministry partners have challenged and encouraged me as I've pursued this writing task, including Brett Payne, Bob Kinzel, Wylie Johnson, Gene Smillie, and many others. I'm also indebted to authors with whom I've had enlightening conversations, including John Piper, Dave Harvey, and Ron Sider. In addition, I'm thankful to the various churches and Bible study groups in which, over the years, I've been able to preach or teach on spiritual formation and receive valuable feedback.

I'm grateful to the team at Biblica Publishing for taking on this project and seeing it through. Volney James has been encouraging from the start and patient with me through a season of ministry transition (he was gracious enough to extend my deadline twice). And the kind, careful help of John Dunham and Kay Larson in refining the book has been very much appreciated.

I would be hard pressed to overstate the importance of the support I've received through God's gift of family. My parents, Ken and Connie Nelson, have been a source of constant affirmation. Cheryl, my beloved wife and best friend and partner in pondering, has supplied much thoughtful input, especially on the urgency of prayer, over the long haul of this writing project. And my children, Elliot, Jeremy, and Emily (in their teens and early twenties), have often blessed me both through their interest in the things I write about and by distracting me from them. I give thanks to the Lord for the blessing of my family.

Chapter 1

TIME AND TIME AGAIN

As a child I'd count the days until Christmas. And not just during December, but for months in advance. Once summer vacation was over, there really wasn't anything else on the calendar worth getting excited about. Now the major appeal of the Christmas season, in my young mind, was the presents. As gifts accumulated under the tree in the weeks leading up to the big day, my anticipation went through the roof. I knew the true meaning of Christmas had to do with Jesus, but still, I was preoccupied with the gifts—what was under that tree, and which packages were for me. The suspense was almost too much to take, waiting for the moment we'd finally tear into all that colorful wrapping paper.

But time changes things, and I had new questions about holiday traditions: how much should we spend, are we inadvertently spreading a consumer mindset to the next generation, and do the gifts upstage the wonder of Christ's birth? Thus holiday merriment was muted by concerns that come with maturity. We may wistfully long for the good old days, a sunny past when life wasn't so complicated. But those days fade, and change is inescapable.

Decades after attending Nathan Hale Elementary School in south Minneapolis, I visited the building and was amazed at how it had shrunk—or so it seemed. Part of our educational experience at Hale School had been the occasional 1960s air-raid drill. We would move swiftly but calmly into the hall, line up in a long row, and bow down toward the wall, putting our hands over our heads so that we could withstand an atom bomb from the Soviets. Such ominous images filled my memory of this school building. But years later I saw the vast, cavernous hallways that had once struck awe into me were now the corridors of a very ordinary building. Time changes things.

The Trouble with Time

So how does the passing of time influence our lives as Christians? The journey of spiritual formation takes us through seasons of the soul.[1] After a stage of initial zeal followed by an episode of eager learning, disenchantment and even bitterness can develop. Pressures and temptations never anticipated in the earlier, simpler seasons of spiritual life eventually confront us. As it is on a long road trip, the journey with Jesus takes many turns, and we can't envision what awaits us around the bend. In particular, we don't foresee where the clash with sin and temptation may take us.

The Apostle Paul pours out his heart for his spiritual "children" in the fourth chapter of Galatians: "I am again in the anguish of childbirth until Christ is formed in you!" The shaping of souls (i.e., the internal life) and the conforming of lifestyles to the pattern of Jesus

---

1. Jim Wilhoit provides a helpful definition of "spiritual formation": "the intentional communal process of growing in our relationship with God and becoming conformed to Christ through the power of the Holy Spirit" (*Spiritual Formation as if the Church Mattered: Growing in Christ through Community* [Grand Rapids: Baker, 2008], 23). While an earlier generation often focused on "Christian education," spiritual formation seeks a more comprehensive work of God in the lives of believers involving heart as well as mind, conduct as well as character, and communal experience as well as personal faith.

are urgent priorities. God has a heart for the Christ-centered spiritual formation of his beloved ones; he intends them to be "conformed to the image of his Son" (Romans 8:29). But sin crops up in countless ways to disrupt and derail progress in our walk with Christ.

This is a book about the ravages of time on the Christian's heart and soul. Putting it that way sounds bleak, and yet I don't want to paint a negative picture; faithfulness to God and his Word prohibits gloom-and-doom thinking. Still, I don't think we evangelical Christians have gone nearly far enough in processing how the life of faith unfolds and morphs over time.[2] And, consequently, we haven't developed certain necessary strategies for persevering in the adventure of discipleship on this long road called "the Christian life."

Consider how in today's Western world we don't have much patience for tasks that take years and years to accomplish. We prefer projects that can be launched and completed within hours or perhaps a few days. Handling lifelong challenges (such as the tension between indwelling sin and progressive sanctification[3]) is very difficult. Among the effects of being immersed in a shortsighted, sound-bite culture is this: we're vulnerable to various theological errors and lopsided spiritual practices that can be combated only by patient, maturing faith over time.

---

2. When I speak of "evangelicals," it's not an activist movement or political bloc that's in view. Rather, I'm thinking of a series of renewals, revivals, and doctrinal corrections aimed at preserving apostolic, New Testament Christianity through the ages. (Cf. John R. W. Stott, *Evangelical Truth* [Downers Grove, IL: InterVarsity Press, 1999], 14–15: "The evangelical faith is not a recent innovation.") Major hallmarks of historic evangelicalism include a high view of Scripture (as inspired, authoritative, and without error), a focus on Jesus Christ as providing the only way of salvation, a call to personal faith and repentance, an emphasis on salvation as a work and gift of God, a charge to draw near to the Lord in practices of personal devotion, and a calling to embrace the Great Commission to make disciples among all people groups.

3. By "indwelling sin" I mean that aspect of human nature that rebels against God. Indwelling sin is a facet of every human's experience. And by "sanctification" I am pointing to the work of God in which he guides us in the process of becoming more and more holy in our conduct.

This book has been simmering in my mind for years. Not only have I strained to make sense of the interplay between sin and spiritual progress in my own life, but again and again, as a pastor and a professor, I've seen the need for insight and God's guidance in this area. There's this unsettled sense in our souls—this discord—that our lives aren't as they should be. Perhaps I've imagined the Christian life to be loftier than it really is, and I should "lighten up." Or perhaps my sinful nature is especially vile and needs to be held under exceptionally strict discipline. Or maybe a key part of the problem is the simple fact that we were made for another world.

George works in the maintenance department of a large hospital— he's a painter. His job is simply to paint every hall and every room on every floor until he finishes the entire building and then to start over and do it again. After all, it takes years to paint the whole facility, and by that time the rooms done first are scuffed and grimy and have outdated colors. So this painter's work is never done. So too, the spiritual labor of seeking the Lord and putting sin to death is perennial. We who know Christ are called into an endless restoration project, a lifelong renovation of our thoughts, passions, and habits. The task is daunting, and yet we proceed with hope, knowing that the Lord is at work within and among us (Philippians 2:13), bringing daily mercies and essential help in time of need (Hebrews 2:18).

To get the big picture, however, we have to remember gains as well as losses that come with the passage of time. For example, over time healthy trees don't just wear down, but they grow deeper in the root, thicker in the trunk, and taller in their branches. Although we never reach spiritual perfection this side of heaven (more will be said about this in the coming pages), by God's grace and with time, we can grow in faith, humility, and wisdom; our stature in terms of godliness can advance even if our bodies are confronted by inevitable declines.

At Longwood Gardens in Kennett Square, Pennsylvania, a cross section of a giant sequoia tree is on exhibit, and the rings of this massive trunk date back to ancient times. Envision a two-thousand-year-old tree. And then, imagine that tree's perspective on the passing of time: the occasional storms, scorching sun, bolts of lightning, wind, and rain—great pressures, to be sure. But the trunk just grows thicker— through the rise and fall of the Roman Empire, during the Middle Ages, into the age of Reformation, on through the Enlightenment and the expansion of European civilization into the "New World," and on into contemporary times. Through the ages the giant sequoia extends its roots deeper and deeper into the soil to get necessary moisture and nutrients, and its branches stretch higher and higher toward the sun's light. Remembering the gains that come with time will help us keep our reflections on the prolonged struggle between sin and sanctification in the proper perspective.

What Is the Problem?

The problem before us is multifaceted, so we'll approach it from several angles. How do we find God's peace in our "unfinished" condition, even as we refuse to make peace with sin? And how do we pace ourselves to finish the race of faith with a pace that's swift and vigorous in pursuit of holiness, yet not so swift that we lose track of our weak, dependent status? The Bible teaches believers to resist temptation and walk in holiness.[4] It also teaches us that we'll still be sinners tomorrow—and every tomorrow until the day we die.[5] How do you manage the tension between what we are called to become and what we must now accept in this world?

I heard a preacher exhorting his people to "slay sin": if the problem is coveting, kill it like you'd kill a bug on the table. But later in the same message he emphasized that we're all sinners—and if you're not sinning now, just wait five seconds. This sermon gave classic expression

---

4. See further chap. 2. Of course, sin wreaks havoc in the lives of non-Christians, but that isn't the focus of this study.
5. On this point, see further chap. 3.

to a mixed message of the church—you will sin, but don't sin; you're a sinner, but stop sinning. How do we put the fact of depravity and the call to holiness together?

To put it differently, the problem ties into the relationship between justification and sanctification. While both involve God's work in people's lives, in justification God declares a person not guilty before the bar of divine justice, while sanctification encompasses the ongoing process of becoming more and more holy—more like Christ. These two works of God go hand in hand, but they aren't the same. The former is decisive and complete the moment it's announced by the Great Judge; he accepts the Son's life as payment covering the penalty for our sin, and we're declared "Not Guilty." But the latter is ongoing. To be sure, it's decisive; he will bring it to completion (Romans 8:29–31; Philippians 1:6). But we actually experience, at best, only a progressive realization of holiness, and progress invariably implies that some measure of sin remains—indwelling sin.

The New Testament shows that God's reign is "now but not yet." We read that "the kingdom of God is in the midst of you" (Luke 17:21) even though Jesus teaches his followers to pray that the kingdom will yet come (Matthew 6:10). This seeming ambiguity can be visualized. Picture the dawn. At dawn it's neither night nor day (daytime is "now but not yet"), but early, faint rays of light confirm that noon's full light is coming. With the appearance of Messiah the reign of God was inaugurated on the earth, even though the final consummation of that reign is yet to come.

We live in what can be described as the overlap of the ages in which the future glory of Christ has, in part, been projected back into the present era. The "ruler of this world" (John 12:31) still rages against the Lord, but his power and time are limited. And one day he'll be banished from our lives with utter finality, and then the Lord will reign without opposition or restraint. That's our grand hope. But for now, we move among the skirmishes between the powers of darkness and the kingdom of light.

And that means we have a problem. These skirmishes aren't just "out there," but right here among God's people, and even within our hearts. We're citizens of heaven yet also exiles in this world—on pilgrimage through the various mountain ranges and dark valleys that make up our days. The Lord has not seen fit to wrap up history yet, and so we continue on the trek with Christ. The problem is, we get it in our heads that the final triumphs of heaven should be ours today; we imagine that pain and loss and sin and failure should be put behind us. But in this overlap of the ages, trials come with the territory. I hope this book will help conscientious Christians come to terms with, and find peace in, God's appointed status for disciples as those who are still "under construction."

Growing but Never Grown Up

Bible interpreters (and that means all of us) have to grapple with complex questions, such as the following: How can various passages call us to holiness and purity while other texts state that we continue to be sinners needing daily confession? How do these different strands of thought in the Bible fit together to form a coherent whole? Are we taught to be and do what we cannot be and do in this life? Further, what about the relationship between grace and law? The Bible (and not just the Old Testament) is full of instructions and demands that we are to follow, but there's also the central theme of grace. How do we take God's commands seriously and not fall into presumption with the misguided excuse, "Well, I can always ask for forgiveness later"? How do we rest in God's grace yet not presume upon his favor? What does God really expect of us here and now?

Our challenge is to understand spiritual maturity's progression through the seasons of life. What does it mean to grow in Christ, to "grow up" spiritually? And is it helpful to imagine growth in terms of attainment? Our physical bodies develop from infancy through childhood and adolescence and on to maturity. It takes time, but eventually we reach the destination; the mature adult is done growing—no more toes squeezed by snug shoes, no more shirtsleeves that strangely don't reach our wrists. But spiritually mature believers never finish advancing in faith and Christlike conduct. What does it mean to be ever growing but never grown up?

Further, what do we make of the claims of many spiritual writers, pastors, and theologians who say that the more you grow as a Christian, the more you realize how much you still need to grow (see chapter 6)? What kind of maturation is it when progress leaves you further away from the goal? This is our quandary: we aren't sure what it really looks like to mature as a disciple in this ambiguous age between the first and second comings of Christ.

The cyclists who compete in the Tour de France churn out amazing times for each segment of the twenty-one-day race around the country. And some stages take competitors high into the Alps. Brutal climbs are followed by exhilarating descents. The average speed for top cyclists in the Tour de France is about forty kilometers per hour.[6] If the Christian life is compared to a race (see chapter 4), how can we find a rhythm of labor and rest in order to be victorious? After all, even Tour de France riders get a couple of days off during the competition.

Similarly, how do we apply the various biblical texts that teach us to rest as well as run? In what ways can a maturing believer live a life of contentment in Christ, and in what ways should we be ever pressing, straining, striving—that is, living a life of discontentment? What does it mean to be a discontent contented Christian? How do we avoid unbiblical perfectionism and yet pursue holiness earnestly? How do

---

6. The 2009 winner, Alberto Contador of Spain, averaged 40.31 km/h over the twenty-one-stage race.

we rest in the Lord and yet do so without falling into complacency or spiritual carelessness? Our challenge is coming to terms with the paradox of restful-yet-restless spirituality.

Straight Talk about Sin

Believers through the ages have grappled with "besetting sins," that is, certain temptations that tap into a Christian's distinctive weaknesses (see further chapter 11). One may be in the grip of racism (and the pride beneath it), or lust, or chronic worry rooted in immature faith, or other sins. Even young Christ-followers who are sensitive to God's Spirit and his Word quickly discover some of their own signature sin struggles. What's more, given our cultural contexts and unique backgrounds, we tend to develop spiritual blind spots—sin ruts we fall into without even realizing it. In this way, each believer develops something of a unique "sin profile," and that means the process of fighting sin and advancing in godliness needs to be tailored to specific individuals and communities.

When a certain pattern of thought or action is seen as normal within a social setting, eventually most people no longer even think about it. My strong hunch, for example, is that there are besetting sins of greed tied to our consumer culture in the West that are all but invisible to many professing Christians. How do we put our finger on such sins—both our individual weaknesses and our corporate vulnerabilities? And then how do we make progress in the fight against such sins? What special measures are necessary to gain an advantage over the unique lure of besetting sins? And (to return to the time factor) why is it so much more difficult to prevail against temptation over the long haul rather than just in a particular instance of pressure?

An honest, if brazen, statement of our situation is this: we're sinners and we'll remain sinners all our days. What's more, the knotty issues of indwelling sin confront every Christian, not just believers whose lives are particularly "messed up"; we all live with sin around us and within us. Although it's true that our sins can be forgiven (1 John 1:9—this is the case for all who trust Jesus Christ for the gift of his saving love), and while it's true that God intends for us to make progress in the battle against sin, we'll still commit sin and be sinners as long as we draw breath this side of heaven. Future sin is a fact of Christian experience.

So the question before us, then is, How should we think, strategize, and act for the earthly journey in light of this reality? How can we plan ahead to live as sinners even while we vehemently refuse to plan to sin? How can we come to terms—indeed, be at peace—with existing as flawed people in a fallen world and yet never declare a truce with sin? I say these things with some "fear and trepidation." My own heart is prone to concoct excuses for sin, and the line between acknowledging the status of sinner and letting down one's guard against sin can be a fine one. We must handle such issues with great care! Still, the Scriptures take us into this delicate territory, and our priority is to follow God's Word.

This book is an attempt to balance biblical realism with biblical hope in a God who can do all things. I believe evangelical Christians have often turned a blind eye to the rugged reality of indwelling sin. And further, sometimes we've preferred pointing fingers at the sins of others. And so, if I'm able in these pages to help readers feel their own ongoing need of daily, free, undeserved, all-sufficient grace from the Lord Jesus Christ (John 15:5), that will have been a valuable accomplishment.

My Journey of Faith

Let me return once more to the time factor. I am a middle-aged American man. I was born at the tail end of the baby boom in 1958, and I was in kindergarten when news of President Kennedy's death stunned our nation (in fact, I remember my teacher receiving a call on her classroom phone, and I vividly recall how she was shaken). I was eleven when Neil Armstrong announced over our thirteen-inch black-and-white television how his one small step had truly been a giant leap for mankind. I graduated from high school in 1976, the year of America's bicentennial, by which time the U.S. government had put an end to the military draft. College and seminary ensued, and in the course of things the Lord led me to my wonderful wife, Cheryl. We were married in 1985 and stepped forward into a life of ministry together.

Cheryl and I were in our early thirties, living in England, when the Berlin wall came down, when Poland's Solidarity movement prevailed, and during Czechoslovakia's Velvet Revolution that brought Vaclav Havel to power (it was a little unnerving for Americans like us to be so close to these tumultuous events, even as we sat in our garden flat in Bristol, looking on via BBC news). On September 11, 2001, at the age of forty-three, I was pastoring a church in the Chicago area. As we canvassed the neighborhood that afternoon with invitations to a community prayer gathering, I remember the mounting lump-in-the-throat feeling as it began to dawn on me that this was Pearl Harbor all over again, only worse since these enemies had attacked civilians. Our world had been rocked, and I was shaken. Welcome to the twenty-first century.

I came to faith in Christ early in that story—at the age of ten. A long and meandering road of discipleship has since taken me into several settings of growth, learning, serving, teaching, writing, leading, and pastoring, and I speak as one whose faith has grown yet also wobbled in various seasons. My message in this book is very much influenced by the realization that easy answers and quick fixes aren't enough in the Christian life. The ravages of time have unearthed various naive, ignorant, and foolish elements of my ever-forming, never-formed spiritual life. I want to make sense of this for myself, and I want to see how others can benefit by reflecting on the issues along with me. I'm seeking to find biblical, God-honoring ways to travel through the decades of this life (if the Lord grants decades), trusting him not only for justification but also for help along the journey of sanctification until I enter into his perfect presence.

And this trek means getting face to face with the reality of sin—my sin, your sin—in ways that have been neglected or even avoided. The Lord God, in his perfect wisdom, has seen fit to save and lead his people in this world in such a way that our spiritual preparation for heaven can take a long time. We can presume that doing things this way was for the best, since, of course, the Lord could have saved us and transported us into glory in a moment. So then, in addition, this book is an exploration of God's good purposes for transforming us into the likeness of his Son gradually rather than instantaneously.

Getting the Big Picture

During a recent summer vacation in Colorado our family visited Copper Mountain. To our surprise, a chair lift at this ski resort was shuttling hikers and mountain bikers high up on the slopes. We took the lift, and it dropped us off up near the tree line though still below the summit. Our plan was to hike to the top, even though this meant a laborious trek at twelve-thousand-some feet where the oxygen gets thin. About two hours later we stood panting atop the world, finally able to look out and take in the stunning sights. What a glorious panorama and what a rich mixture of colors—green slopes, patches of snow on gray stone, shafts of sunlight breaking through scattered clouds, and all against the backdrop of a deep blue sky.

What struck me was how different things looked from above. During the climb our attention was focused mostly on the next step and the terrain nearby. But from the top we were finally able to stop, look up, and get the big picture. We saw the highway that had brought us to Copper Mountain, as well as other roads and various mountain peaks and ranges in the distance. We could see the path our family had followed up from the place the chair lift unloaded. Things came into perspective.

So it is in the journey with Christ. That is, it takes time, and it takes many turns in the path, countless obstacles on the trail, and long years of discipleship before the big panorama begins to come clear. With time and experience, by God's help, as we advance in faith and draw closer and closer into his glorious presence, we can begin to see the big picture of spiritual formation.

On the Right Track

I'm grateful for a wide array of Christian leaders who take the Bible seriously and therefore grapple earnestly with sin and sanctification. They're dedicated evangelical pastors, teachers, authors, musicians, and ministry leaders who've ably led large sectors of the Christian community and guarded them from theological decline, moral compromise, and the reduction of faith into some convenient device in life's tool kit. Their churches stand out as fellowships where people meet Christ, the Bible is taught with clarity and boldness, and believers desire and receive help to grow strong in faith.

These spiritual leaders are on the right track. They're the bane of nominal "Christianity" and all complacent reactions to Jesus. Their books deliver penetrating critiques of "cheap grace" and of religious hypocrisy into which we're prone to fall. Their parachurch ministries are known for creative and courageous strategies to confront our troubled world, directing the truth of Christ and his saving love toward lost and hurting souls. It's in such God-seeking circles that I've gained insight and inspiration, and I'm very thankful the Lord has led me in this way.

This book, built on a platform of such gratitude, nevertheless delivers a challenge to all those wonderful churches, schools, ministries, and movements that are so important within evangelicalism for taking

Christ seriously and aspiring to bring all of life, every shred of it, under his lordship. And yet, in my sincere thankfulness, I need to walk a fine line. Although I am deeply convinced from Scripture that these Christian leaders are on the right track, along with their passion for Christ and zeal for the godliness of his people come certain "occupational hazards." In particular, with the quest for holiness comes the perennial risk that some would suppose they're being pushed toward an unattainable perfection. Further, on occasion these outstanding Christian leaders make statements or arouse a spiritual momentum that can be misunderstood—that can be taken as a summons to a height of experience that in fact is beyond our reach today.

A. W. Tozer's book *The Pursuit of God* provides a classic expression of spiritual passion. "The moment the Spirit has quickened us to life in regeneration our whole being senses its kinship to God and leaps up in joyous recognition. That is the heavenly birth without which we cannot see the Kingdom of God. It is, however, not an end but an inception, for now begins the glorious pursuit, the heart's happy exploration of the infinite riches of the Godhead. That is where we begin, I say, but where we stop no man has yet discovered, for there is in the awful and mysterious depths of the Triune God neither limit nor end."[7] Tozer's vision of seeking God is exhilarating, and, if rightly understood, profoundly helpful.

I've appreciated the writings and messages of numerous dedicated Christian leaders on the pursuit of godliness and spiritual formation that involves taking on the character of Christ, the life of prayer, rigorous study of Scripture, and the consistent application of God's truth and love in all facets of life, including work and careers, marriage and singleness, love and sex, finances and lifestyle, the active engagement of believers as salt and light within their communities, and the sending of Christian witnesses to the ends of the earth in order to make disciples among all people groups. Do you remember WWJD? It was

---

7. A. W. Tozer, *The Pursuit of God* (Harrisburg, PA: Christian Publications, 1948), 14.

a fad with some simplistic applications, but the basic question was valid: what would Jesus do? And how are we to conduct our lives in this world to follow in his steps? However, we should also ask how patterning our lives on the model of Christ can lead to misguided ambitions and unnecessary discouragement.

When I think of authors who call people to wholehearted devotion to Christ, a flood of names runs through my mind, followed immediately by thanks to God for their works. To be sure, they don't all have the same emphases, and they've influenced me in various different ways. The common thread is a vigorous defense of what I'll call "serious Christianity" (and by "serious" I don't mean sternness but wholeheartedness in embracing all that the Bible teaches)—no pretense, no putting on a show, and no going through church motions because "it's what we do."

Dallas Willard raises the banner of fervent discipleship in various writings, including his essays in *The Great Omission*. Many Christians are disappointed in their faith; what they profess just isn't working. "There is an obvious Great Disparity between, on the one hand, the *hope for life expressed in Jesus*—found real in the Bible and in many shining examples from among his followers—and, on the other hand, the *actual day-to-day behavior, inner life, and social presence* of most of those who now profess adherence to him."[8] The "great omission" is the neglect of discipleship in Christian teaching, and it's this that gives root to the "great disparity." The influence of Bonhoeffer's call to discipleship and assault on "cheap grace" runs deep in Willard's works.

Similarly, in *My Heart—Christ's Home*, Robert Boyd Munger shows how foolish and harmful it is to try to keep Jesus away from any "closet" in our lives: he intends to come in and take up residence in all corners of one's life. But might we create unreachable expectations by

---

8. Dallas Willard, *The Great Omission: Reclaiming Jesus' Essential Teaching on Discipleship* (San Francisco: Harper, 2006), x, emphasis in original.

calling believers to practice total devotion? And what kinds of spiritual fallout are there when such expectations are repeatedly not met?

I have tremendous appreciation for John Piper and his ministry proclaiming God's Word. In the 1980s Cheryl and I worshiped and ministered at Bethlehem Baptist Church in Minneapolis, where John pastored and still serves. We were married there, and for several years we had an active role in the church's international student outreach. I held an interim pastoral staff position at Bethlehem from 1986 to 1987. It's been over twenty years since we've lived in the Minneapolis area, but whenever we travel to be with family there, we're always eager to visit Bethlehem. John's sermons, poems, articles, conference messages, and various books, together with his "blood earnest" demeanor, have made a profound impression on me—an impact for which I am deeply grateful. And yet I wonder if, at times, while aiming for lofty heights, we may need help to keep down-to-earth realities of today's Christian life in view.[9]

Over the years I've gotten more and more interested in various Puritan authors, and reading their works has often been like a breath of fresh air to me. J. I. Packer compares these bold, Bible-centered, God-focused believers to redwood trees—giants in spiritual and theological stature.[10] Reading them feels like cutting through life's clutter and chaos and finding words that matter. I have especially appreciated Richard Sibbes on the believer's interior life, Thomas Watson's *All Things for Good* (a treatise on Romans 8:28), *The Rare Jewel of Christian Contentment* by Jeremiah Burroughs, *Precious Remedies against Satan's Devices* by Thomas Brooks, and John Owen's classic work *Sin and Temptation*. These authors demonstrate that "true religion" is serious

---

9. Piper has also made vital contributions to the quest for an honest, biblical spirituality that both aspires to honor the Lord in all things *and* grapples with the fact of indwelling sin (see especially his book *Spectacular Sins and Their Global Purpose in the Glory of Christ* [Wheaton: Crossway, 2008]).

10. J. I. Packer, *A Quest for Godliness: The Puritan Vision of the Christian Life* (Wheaton: Crossway, 1990), 11–12.

yet also joyful, rigorous yet also exhilarating. At the same time, the careless caricature of the Puritans as stern and stuffy men shows that it's quite possible to misconstrue their vision of the Christian life. How do we take proper encouragement from them and yet avoid being overwhelmed by lofty expectations?

In similar ways I have been greatly stretched and strengthened through the writings of Jonathan Edwards. His seventy resolutions, written when he was about twenty years old, convey a sense of utter abandon to the Lord, a zeal to make every last word, every breath, an act of devotion to his all-glorious King. (E.g., Number 4: "Resolved, never to do any manner of thing, whether in soul or body, less or more, but what tends to the glory of God; nor be, nor suffer it, if I can avoid it.") In *Religious Affections* Edwards successfully demonstrates that genuine Christian experience engages not just the mind but also the heart: the whole of one's being is caught up in the wonder of knowing Christ as Savior and Lord. Correspondingly, the absence of a heart moved by the grace and greatness of the Lord signals a lack of genuine faith. But how do we apply this elevated spiritual vision in light of our feeble, faltering hearts?

To shift gears somewhat, many vibrant and growing churches I know of are fellowships in which bold steps are taken to help people submit all of life to Christ. Pastors don't tiptoe around sensitive parishioners, making sure not to offend them, nor are they looking for ways to accommodate the wishes of an unbelieving world. Preaching and teaching embrace the Bible in its parts and as a whole, worship and prayer are given high priority, small groups provide personal support and accountability, and ministry teams apply the gospel to various needs in the community and around the world. The church-as-social-club mindset is rejected in these fellowships, in keeping with Tozer's admonition to "go hard after God."

Harvest Bible Chapel in suburban Chicago, where James MacDonald pastors, comes to mind. He speaks a penetrating, no-nonsense message confronting sin and calling for faithful devotion. Along similar lines, Mark Driscoll, pastor of Mars Hill Church in Seattle and a prominent conference speaker and author, is well known for bold and uncompromising messages, even if it means taking other Christians to task for softening or dodging the Bible's hard statements. In addition, the recent recanting of the seeker-driven ministry mantra by Bill Hybels and the Willow Creek team deserves mention. They've seen that whole and healthy Christians are those who grow strong in faith and the knowledge of Christ; it's not enough to bring in large numbers for nonthreatening Sunday services.[11]

Jim Cymbala at the Brooklyn Tabernacle, through *Fresh Wind, Fresh Fire* (and other works), has called believers back to prayer and reminded them to hope in God for powerful life transformation. Henry Blackaby's *Experiencing God* materials confront tentative Christians with the need to make faith practical and attempt God-sized tasks. And thanks to Rick Warren, the "purpose driven church" movement has forced congregations to look in the mirror, filter out extraneous practices, and develop ministries that fit under five vital biblical headings: worship, fellowship, discipleship, ministry, and evangelism. This, in turn, has often been a key ingredient in revitalizing churches for a focused, Bible-based ministry.

I could say more—about Billy Graham's Spirit-anointed message the last night of Urbana '79, summoning God's people to step forward with unwavering readiness for mission; about Elisabeth Elliot's bold witness and radical discipleship demonstrated in her life and recounted in her writings; about the Passion Conference movement (involving Louie Giglio, Beth Moore, John Piper, and others) and its momentum for worship and vigilant discipleship; and about Mark Dever and the "9Marks" ministry focusing on glorifying God in the local church. I could go on and on—those I've named represent a wide

---

11. See, e.g., "Willow Creek Repents?" posted on Oct. 18, 2007, at http://blog.christianitytoday.com/outofur/archives/2007/10/willow_creek_re.html.

and wonderful stream of evangelical leadership, and I thank the Lord for them. But I return to the question: With such grand aspirations, might believers be at risk of expecting too much of heavenly glory in this era when the sun of God's reign is still just dawning?

Additionally, Christian music often issues a call to radical devotion, and much "vertical" music (i.e., with lyrics addressing God) expresses the believer's zeal and affection for Christ. For example, the eighth-century Irish hymn "Be Thou My Vision" cries out to God that day and night he'd fill one's vision, thoughts, and affections; it's a prayer for comprehensive spiritual transformation. In much contemporary music, sights are also set high: "You are the air I breathe," "You are my all in all," "I could sing of your love forever," "We will praise you all of our days," and so on. These are ambitious declarations of full allegiance. As with a great deal of Christian preaching, teaching, and writing, these excellent songs articulate a serious spirituality, a devout and earnest response to Christ as Lord. But in our frailty, how do we handle such bold, heavenward hopes—how do we sing these songs without confusing present reality and future glory?

Help for Imperfect Christians

Despite all the wonderful seriousness of these pacesetting evangelical leaders and their vital messages, this book issues a challenge to all such presentations of the Christian life. Not because I believe they're wrong—not at all. They're the only hope for the wider visible church and for our desperate world. The leaders who call for thoroughgoing devotion to Christ are on the right track of being faithful to the Word of God, and their ministries and spiritual leadership are most commendable.

But in the quest to give God our all, we need help. At the high altitude of these invigorating vistas, the notions of spiritual formation and the Christian life that people come away with can be askew or incomplete. The elephant in the room is ongoing sin in the life of every believer. What do we mean by singing that we're giving God our all when we know full well that we have failed and will fail at doing this? What's really in our minds when we tell Christians not to yield to temptation but to obey and walk in holiness and imitate God and be like Jesus (etc.) when we know, from experience and from the Bible, they'll stumble and have mixed success at best?

My concern is that, through well-intended yet perhaps insufficiently nuanced exhortations to lead God-honoring lives, we can set believers up for unnecessary confusion and even disillusionment. The impact of the serious gospel on sincere Christians is, potentially, to generate expectations that can't be met this side of heaven—great expectations of glorious lives. The remedy for this problem, of course, is not to water down God's truth but to help believers grapple with the full array of that truth, including the interplay of elements having to do with indwelling sin and progressive sanctification.

Let me say plainly that the last thing I want to do is to make excuses for sin or to give the impression that it doesn't really matter if we give in to temptation ("After all, no one reaches perfection this side of heaven"). That would just mean swinging the pendulum from one problem to another, and we'd simply end up with a different misunderstanding of the biblical message. Those who proclaim a rigorous discipleship are definitely on the right track. The kind of correction needed isn't a "U-turn" but a subtle maneuvering to avoid perfectionism or triumphalism, yet away from despair over sinful failings.

We need a spiritual theology, grounded in biblical wisdom and discernment, that comes to terms with remaining sin while still seeking gains in godliness from a stance of humble faith. Similarly, believers need to find a way to plan ahead for life tomorrow and the next day in which they will be sinners, yet to do so without planning to sin. This is a delicate balance, and it is the underlying concern to be addressed in the pages ahead.

Part One

BIBLICAL FOUNDATIONS

Chapter 2

AIMING HIGH:

THE CALL TO HOLINESS

The world record for the high jump is 2.45 meters (just over eight feet), which was set by Javier Sotomayor of Cuba in 1993. To visualize this feat in an everyday setting, we might imagine someone leaping from one floor right up to the next in a two-story house. The vast majority of people, of course, can't come close to this achievement. Typical able-bodied adults have to make an effort just to touch the ceiling. The difference between the high-jumping skill level of the average person and that of Javier Sotomayor in his prime is simply enormous. To say that "the bar has been set high" is a drastic understatement.

Be Holy as I Am Holy!

The Scriptures envision a God-exalting spiritual life that sets the bar very high—as high as it could be: "For I am the Lord your God. Consecrate yourselves therefore, and be holy, for I am holy" (Leviticus 11:44). The very holiness of God is put forth as the standard for believers to meet. And not only were the Israelites called to reflect divine holiness, but the same is true for followers of Christ in the new covenant era. This continuity is expressed in 1 Peter 1:15–16: "As he who called you is holy, you also be holy in all your conduct, since it is written, 'You shall be holy, for I am holy.'"

For the apostle Peter such holiness is not an abstract, theoretical notion but an intensely practical matter. It involves disciplining the mind and placing one's hope fully in the grace of God, and it's expressed in obedience to the Lord—that is, by refusing to follow "the passions of your former ignorance" (1 Peter 1:13–14). This isn't an ethereal vision but a true-to-life calling to godly action and moral purity. What's more, it extends to the full range of experience: be holy "in all your conduct." Do so *in all of life.* Yes, the bar is set very high.

At this point we might read on in 1 Peter, anticipating qualifying remarks about being holy "to the best of your ability" or "increasingly over time." "Be as holy as possible." After all, experience shows that nobody's perfect, and that certainly includes those who aspire to imitate God and follow in Jesus' steps. But the blunt command is delivered without qualification: *Be holy in all your conduct.* The analogy of high jumping begins to break down, in fact, since in that case at least one person has successfully reached the incredibly lofty standard of eight feet. When it comes to being holy in all of our conduct, and doing so consistently over time, however, no one can claim to have measured up. To do so would be like high jumping over the Empire State Building. An honest look in the mirror—and careful attention to God's Word—makes this evident. Who can claim to have a flawless record of holiness in thoughts, words, and deeds? So the reader of Scripture is left wondering what to do with 1 Peter 1:15–16.

And so, too, with numerous other passages and the major biblical themes they support. Even a cursory glance elsewhere in the Bible reveals a great many texts that set the bar of spiritual practice exceedingly high. The Christian's attitude should be like that of Jesus Christ, depicted in the second chapter of Philippians, who humbly set aside his own privileges and embraced the way of service, pouring out his life for others. Believers are to follow in the steps of the One who committed no sin (1 Peter 2:21–22; Hebrews 4:15).

The believer's thoughts, attitudes, words, and deeds are all to be God-honoring. The mind is to be filled with whatever is true, honorable, just, pure, lovely, gracious, excellent, and praiseworthy (Philippians 4:8). There's no room for compromise: "But sexual immorality and all impurity or covetousness must not even be named among you, as is proper among saints" (Ephesians 5:3).

Speech serves as a practical example here. Christians are to speak so that "no corrupting talk" comes out of their mouths, but only words that build up and spread grace (Ephesians 4:29). Our speech should "always be gracious, seasoned with salt, so that you may know how you ought to answer each person" (Colossians 4:6). This high calling for speech is put forward without qualification; batting .500 might be outstanding in baseball, but a 50 percent success rate in godly speech does not begin to meet these biblical standards. As the psalmist says, "I will bless the LORD at all times; his praise shall continually be in my mouth" (34:1).

Further, right words must be matched by holy actions: "And whatever you do, in word or deed, do everything in the name of the Lord Jesus, giving thanks to God the Father through him" (Colossians 3:17). Paul's prayer for the Colossians is that "you may be filled with the knowledge of his will in all spiritual wisdom and understanding, so as to walk in a manner worthy of the Lord, fully pleasing to him, bearing fruit in every good work and increasing in the knowledge of God" (1:9–10). Of course, the disciples set the bar in the clouds because Jesus himself did: "You shall love the Lord your God with all your heart and with all your soul and with all your mind" (Mark 12:30). Devotion is to be complete, not partial.

"On Earth as It Is in Heaven"

In his model prayer in Matthew 6, Jesus teaches his disciples to pray to the Father that his kingdom would come and his will be done on earth as in heaven. This appeal for "heaven on earth" expresses the loftiest of spiritual hopes. Think what's entailed in pleading for God's will to be realized in ways that match the perfections of heaven! Imagine the implications, say, for attitudes (no place for doubt, fear, pride, or any other self-centered ways), conversations (no more criticism, lying, flattery, distortion, use of "spin"), moral conduct (no more wandering eyes or hoarding of goods for oneself), and God-centered, joyful life in the body of believers (no discord, no gossip, no maneuvering or manipulating for personal gain, no competition for influence or prominence). *No more* of such things—that would be a taste of heaven on earth!

What's more, the phrase "on earth as it is in heaven" relates to all three lines before it. That is, we pray that three things would take place on earth the same way they transpire in heaven: (1) the hallowing of God's name (i.e., reverent, earnest praise); (2) the exercise of God's kingly reign; and (3) the doing of the Lord's will. This is a prayer driven by God's agenda, a heart cry of wonder as one gazes upon almighty God in all his grandeur. Believers whose prayers sound more like a modest grocery list ("I could use a new supply of this earthly comfort and another dose of that temporal convenience") than a plea for heaven on earth need to stop and absorb the radical vision of Matthew 6:9–10!

An important question sometimes bypassed is *when*. Are we asking God to wrap up history and bring about this grand praise with the return of Christ and the end of the age? Is this petition equivalent to saying, "Maranatha!" ("Our Lord, come!")? Or is this a request for powerful divine intervention here and now, in the thick of life as we know it today, to transform our experience even before the coming of the end?

Though some interpreters argue for an "eschatological" orientation to the Lord's Prayer (i.e., that "thy kingdom come" is essentially a plea for the Lord's return), the most plausible reading of the text is that we're to ask the Father to penetrate *today's world* with outposts of his praise and beachheads of his glorious will and reign. The main reason for saying this is the prayer's literary context: in the surrounding chapters, followers of Christ are taught new ethical and spiritual priorities for their present lives, for example, the facing of persecution, being salt and light in the world, applying the law to matters of the heart (e.g., anger or lust), not retaliating against but loving enemies, not giving, praying, or fasting for a human audience, not hoarding earthly treasures, and learning from the birds and lilies to say no to anxiety. In short, one is hard pressed to escape the implications of context: Matthew 6:10 conveys hope for the life of discipleship in the present time.[1] Further, when the eschatological age does come into view in the seventh chapter, it's to warn people to respond rightly to Jesus as they follow him *today*, thus preparing for future judgment.

It would be less demanding, in terms of practical Christian living, if the Lord's Prayer were focused on the life to come. That is, it would be easier to imagine the reign and will of God being achieved in heaven-like ways in the coming age of final and total divine conquest than in the present tumultuous world in which adversarial powers are still allowed to operate. But that reduces the prayer to an appeal for the obvious: "Make life glorious when we enter into glory; make heaven heavenly." And so, we press forward to interpret the plea for "heaven on earth" for the present age.

---

1. So Jeffrey B. Gibson, "Matthew 6:9–13//Luke 11:2–4: An Eschatological Prayer?", *BTB* 31 (2001): 96–105. See also Craig Blomberg, *Matthew* (NAC 22; Nashville: Broadman, 1992), 119; Robert H. Gundry, *Matthew: A Commentary on His Literary and Theological Art* (Grand Rapids: Eerdmans, 1982), 106–7.

A Life Fully Pleasing to God

Many other New Testament passages also teach or clearly imply that Christians are to lead godly, holy, Christlike lives here and now. Here are a few examples:

- The Son pleads with the Father that future believers—Christians through the ages—would be one even as the Son and Father are one (John 17:20–23). Such an elevated standard for the quality of relationships among believers is staggering—our unity is to be on a par with the oneness experienced within the Godhead!

- Believers are exhorted to cleanse themselves from every kind of bodily and spiritual defilement, completing a life of holiness (2 Corinthians 7:1).

- Believers are to lead lives worthy of God and to please him (Colossians 1:9–10; cf. Ephesians 4:1).

- God's people are to be "competent, equipped for every good work" through Scripture, which is inspired by God and profitable for instruction (2 Timothy 3:16–17).

- With the God of peace through Jesus Christ, believers are equipped with "everything good that you may do his will, working in us that which is pleasing in his sight" (Hebrews 13:21).

- Trials allow believers' faith to be tested, toward the end "that you may be perfect and complete, lacking in nothing" (James 1:2–4).

- Believers are to follow the example of Christ and live no longer in this life by human passions but by the will of God (1 Peter 4:1–2; 2:21).

- God's "divine power has granted to us all things that pertain to life and godliness" (2 Peter 1:3).

These broad statements underscore the fact that *all aspects of life* (including thoughts, attitudes, words, and deeds) are to be fully devoted to God's honor. Again, absent from such passages are qualifying remarks about being summoned to halfway obedience or occasional holiness.

"I Am Writing . . . to You So That You May Not Sin"

The apostle John pauses in 1 John 2:1 to make explicit a reason for writing to his Christian readers: "My little children, I am writing these things to you so that you may not sin." Although he goes on to say that Christ will act as advocate before the Father if anyone does sin, John's desire is that believers would not commit acts of sin. Stated positively, this would mean John's readers are to "walk" in the same way Jesus did (2:6). Similarly, John's Gospel relays Jesus' call to the disciples to imitate his self-giving service and love, as he demonstrated by washing their feet. The risen Jesus then goes on to say, "As the Father has sent me, even so I am sending you" (20:21).

The lofty expectation of Christlike conduct and holy living is brought out by John with even greater emphasis elsewhere: "No one who abides in him sins; no one who sins has either seen him or known him" (1 John 3:6 rsv). "No one born of God commits sin; for God's nature abides in him, and he cannot sin because he is born of God" (3:9 rsv). Now, to be sure, there are questions about how to render the Greek present tense in these verses: "to sin" or "to keep on sinning" (the latter bringing out the progressive element often intended with the present tense). The esv and niv have "keeps on sinning," while the rsv and nrsv simply read "sin." The statement in 3:9 that the believer "cannot" sin is so strong that, in light of 1:8–10 (see further chapter 3), it's best to infer that John has the present-progressive sense in mind in 3:6 and 3:9: "to keep on sinning." But even so, when linked with 2:1, 2:6, John 13:35, and John 20:21, there remains an extremely elevated vision and challenge in John's writings that Christian conduct should conform to the highest standards, namely to the practice of Jesus Christ himself.

The spiritual and moral trajectory of the New Testament reaches its apex in Ephesians 5:1–2: "Therefore be imitators of God, as beloved children. And walk in love, as Christ loved us and gave himself up for us, a fragrant offering and sacrifice to God." The call to Christlike love is paired here with this brief but breathtaking charge: *Be imitators of God.* The Lord calls us to exhibit a family likeness as his children! And again, there's no qualification suggesting we might be satisfied with partial or general or progressive godliness.

One can hardly accuse the New Testament of settling for some status quo religiosity or a modest spiritual improvement program. Nor is the summons to godliness presented as wishful thinking, since it's brought out in Ephesians that God is able to do within and among his people far more abundantly than all we ask or think (3:20; cf. Philippians 2:12–13). God is powerful beyond description and thus able to accomplish unbelievable feats within the lives of his people individually and corporately. This is a source of vital hope when considering the high calling of the Christian life.

Able to Escape Temptation?

God's enabling power deserves further attention: you or I may not be able to leap over the Empire State Building on our own strength, but all things are possible with God. Can we look to God for strength to be holy in all we do? Divine power and the ability of believers are both addressed in a well-known biblical promise, 1 Corinthians 10:13: "No temptation has overtaken you that is not common to man. God is faithful, and he will not let you be tempted beyond your ability, but with the temptation he will also provide the way of escape, that you may be able to endure it." Careful attention to this key text can help us find the pathway toward holiness.[2]

Several absolute statements here encourage the Christian reader: *No* believer faces unprecedented temptations, but rather *all* face various common enticements inherent within human experience. Further, because "God is faithful" (i.e., faithful to his many promises to protect and provide for his people), he won't let any believer face unbearable pressure to sin. The Lord will certainly provide a "way of escape," that is, some avenue, some alternative path, by which Christians may turn away from sin when temptation strikes.

Further, Paul emphatically points out that, as a result of God's provision, believers are *able* to endure temptations without falling. The Lord "will not let you be tempted beyond your *ability*" (emphasis added); when temptation comes, God will provide a way of escape "that you may be *able* to endure it" (emphasis added). Twice the verb "(you) are able" is applied to Christians: as a result of God's help, believers can withstand temptation. It seems, then, that 1 Corinthians 10:13 teaches that the Christian is able not to sin. And yet, there are follow-up questions: Is this notion in keeping with what's taught in the wider context of 1 Corinthians and Paul's other letters? Further, if it's true that Christians are able not to sin, why is it that history and experience provide no examples of sinless believers?

In this passage Paul surrounds the invitation to hope with words of warning. In fact, 1 Corinthians 10:13 is bracketed by commands highlighting the real threat and danger of sin. The memory of idolatry, immorality, and grumbling by Israel's wilderness generation is sharply applied to the Corinthian Christians: don't be so sure you'll withstand temptation's pressure, for an attitude of self-assurance may lead directly to a fall (10:12). By implication, then, Paul charges his readers to be humbly aware of their weaknesses when temptation beckons.

---

2. See further my paper "Discipleship Dissonance" (available at http://sinandspiritual-formation.blogspot.com).

Further, in 10:14 Paul adds an exhortation to flee from sin while clinging to the sure promise that God will provide a way to escape temptation's pull: "Therefore, my beloved, flee from idolatry." The use of "therefore" to link verses 13 and 14 is especially significant—God's promise of a way of escape is no reason to take temptation lightly. On the contrary, believers are urged to be vigilant and resist sin's allure *because* help is promised to them. A reading of 10:13 that makes sense within its literary context, then, is one that keeps the urgent warnings of verses 12 and 14 in view.

Lifeguards at the Jersey Shore are keenly aware of dangerous rip currents. Each summer tragic stories unfold when careless swimmers disregard beach regulations and wander where powerful riptides can pull them out to sea. In some cases, no amount of swimming against the riptide's force can bring a person to safety; in fact, trying to swim in against a current that's rushing out is a sure way to become exhausted. A wiser response to the rip current's deadly power is to swim parallel to the shore until you escape its pull. So too, finding the way of escape from temptation involves taking warnings seriously. Safety is found only by those who have a proper "fear" of sin and a humble heart that longs to receive the Lord's loving correction.

Regarding the time frame of the temptations in view in 10:13, a variety of interpretations have been proposed. But for those who correctly link the text with the temptations of daily Christian experience rather than final judgment,[3] it's recognized that being given a way of escape is no guarantee that one will follow it. It's best, rather, to take the promise of a way of escape as indicating that *in any given instance* when the believer turns to the Lord in humble trust, he or

---

3. See, e.g., Richard B. Hays, *First Corinthians* (Interpretation; Louisville: John Knox Press, 1997), 166; Ben Witherington III, *Conflict and Community in Corinth: A Socio-Rhetorical Commentary on 1 and 2 Corinthians* (Carlisle: Paternoster, 1995), 224; Anthony Thiselton, *The First Epistle to the Corinthians* (NIGTC; Grand Rapids: Eerdmans, 2000), 748–49. By contrast, an eschatological reading of 10:13 stumbles over the explicit focus on present-time temptations in vv. 12 and 14.

she will receive strength to resist temptation's pull (cf. Hebrews 2:18; 4:14–16).

The ability in view in 1 Corinthians 10:13 is then experienced in connection with the exercise of active faith that "takes heed" (v. 12) and "flees" from sin (v. 14). The comforts of verse 13 don't invite believers to let down their guard or fall back on the presumption that their ability is sufficient to withstand all threats. Rather, the reassurance offered should inspire Christians to receive the warnings of verses 12 and 14 with eager humility, so that by acting boldly in faith to follow Christ and resist temptation, they will be able, in any situation in which they so act, to endure under pressure and say no to sin.[4]

Ephesians 3:20 is another important text on God's power at work in our lives. We're assured that God "is able to do immeasurably more than all we ask or imagine, according to his power that is at work within us" (NIV). In light of such a grand declaration, we mustn't underestimate the Lord's benevolent and powerful intentions. Similarly, verse 24 of Jude offers this benediction: "To him who is able to keep you from falling and to present you before his glorious presence without fault and with great joy" (NIV). "Falling" here has moral connotations—falling into sin. The Lord is able to keep us from that misery.

The thrust of these various passages about the ability of God at work in and for believers is to inspire hope and encourage faith that generate Christlike conduct.[5] However, as with 1 Corinthians 10:13, we must be careful not to read into such texts any kind of invitation to be careless with respect to the serious and insidious dangers that come with temptations to sin.

---

4. Cf. Tim Chester, *You Can Change: God's Transforming Power for Our Sinful Behavior and Negative Emotions* (Wheaton: Crossway, 2010), 175. (Sin is never inevitable, but it is inevitable that I'll continue to sin: "The truth is that I'm not bound to commit any particular sin, but I still make choices to sin because my desires have not been completely transformed.")
5. See also Eph. 1:19; Phil. 2:13; 2 Peter 1:3.

The Lordship of Jesus Christ

In the end, it's indisputable that the Lord calls his people to practice holy living. The charge is not to be somewhat godly; we're never summoned to aim at partial holiness. This biblical call to God-honoring excellence is clear, and its applications are far-reaching. Such a vision of spiritual life is striking for how it stands apart from various nominal and compartmentalized religious practices that are widespread in our day. Failing to take the call to holiness seriously may seem to make life easier, but it's not a solution the Scriptures can tolerate.

Another mistaken "solution" to the way the Bible sets the bar high is to imagine that such standards apply only to a spiritual elite—to some inner circle of advanced Christians who have a loftier standing than the mainstream believing population. In fact, the various texts that commission readers to walk in holiness are clearly directed to believers and churches in general. "Be holy" is a charge to all Christians; the urging to imitate God is an admonition to the church.

In the late 1980s and early 1990s, an effort to portray holiness as essential only for a spiritual elite surfaced in the "Lordship Salvation" debate. The timeless question was whether or not authentic Christian faith necessarily recognized Christ as Lord. Was it enough to receive Jesus as Savior? Could you truly believe and yet say, "No, thanks," to Christ's lordship and the pursuit of holiness?[6] My sense is that there was a good amount of rhetorical fireworks and misunderstanding in this debate (e.g., the term "believe" was used in different ways by different authors). After cutting through the distractions, however, the case from the Scriptures for trusting Jesus Christ as Savior *and* Lord seems compelling. Relegating lordship to the category of what's "optional" is to fail to recognize Jesus Christ for who he is.[7]

---

6. See Ron Julian's work, *Righteous Sinners: The Believer's Struggle with Faith, Grace, and Works* (Colorado Springs: NavPress, 1998), for a helpful discussion of the Lordship Salvation debate (e.g., 19–23).

7. So too John Piper, *Finally Alive: What Happens When We Are Born Again* (Ross-shire,

Of course, this is not to concede to any form of legalism or "works righteousness." Holy conduct is surely not presented in the Scriptures as a means of deserving God's favor, but rather as the natural and grateful response to his saving intervention we've *already* experienced.[8] Further, the necessity of accepting the lordship of Christ is rooted in the thoughtful recognition that the Bible speaks of believing in Jesus (i.e., faith in Jesus) as practical trust. Faith is not mere assent to facts about Jesus but also personal allegiance and dependence. And such practical trust shows itself in deeds of obedience. Galatians 5:6, for example, emphasizes "faith working through love." In other words, faith has practical effects; the absence of tangible evidence of trust suggests the absence of authentic faith. Of course, this does not mean that believers suddenly become perfect in their conduct, but rather that by faith they enter into a new way of life. This life has new hopes, new incentives, and new thankfulness. These are natural and inevitable when one embraces Jesus Christ, who's both Savior and Lord in relation to his children. After all, faith without works is dead—it is not real faith. Without holiness no one will see the Lord (Hebrews 12:14).[9]

The Beauty of Holiness

El Capitan is a granite wall half a mile high jutting up from the valley floor of Yosemite National Park. Climbers look at this magnificent stone face and can't resist the challenge. The first free climb of El Capitan (i.e., without artificial aids to help in the ascent—using ropes only for protection from falling) took place in 1988 when Todd Skinner and Paul Piana made the ascent over a nine-day period. Since

---

Scotland: Christian Focus, 2009), 15, 62, 72, 189.

8. It's the "obedience of faith"—i.e., resulting from faith (Rom. 1:5; 16:26; cf. James 2:14–26).

9. Cf. John Piper, "Letter to a Friend concerning the So-called 'Lordship Salvation'" in *The Pleasures of God* (Portland: Multnomah, 1991), 279–305.

then, various records have been set for free and aided climbs. In 2005 Tommy Caldwell free-climbed El Capitan twice in one day.[10] Tall pine trees in the Yosemite Valley look like the nap of carpeting from a perch high on this stone wall. Cloud systems sometimes pass entirely beneath mountaineers well on their way up on the granite face. El Capitan provides a parable of majesty—the sheer size, its stunning beauty, the sense of smallness you feel in the presence of its looming magnificence.

The Scriptures paint a spectacular picture of the Lord God, who is majestic in holiness. The seraphs call out praises of the Most High as they fly: "Holy, holy, holy is the Lord Almighty; the whole earth is full of his glory" (Isaiah 6:3 NIV). To say that God is holy is to underscore his matchless purity; it's a way of articulating something of his breathtaking splendor. The hymn text by John S. B. Monsell gives words to this praise:

> O worship the Lord in the beauty of holiness!
> Bow down before Him, His glory proclaim;
> With gold of obedience, and incense of lowliness,
> Kneel and adore Him: the Lord is His Name![11]

The Scriptures summon believers to stand in awe before the Lord and then to reflect his radiant holiness in the church and to the world. Our privilege is to fix our eyes on Jesus Christ, the Son of God, who is "the radiance of God's glory and the exact representation of his being" (Hebrews 1:3 NIV), and then, in humble and joyful gratitude, to shine his brilliant light upon our neighbors and among all the people groups on earth. The Scriptures will have more to say on matters of sin and sanctification, but the responsible handling of the whole counsel of God we pursue in these pages must never diminish this staggering call to Christlike, Christ-exalting holiness.

---

10. Source: http://en.wikipedia.org/wiki/El_Capitan.
11. Source: http://www.cyberhymnal.org/htm/o/w/oworship.htm.

Chapter 3

FALLING DOWN:
THE FACT OF INDWELLING SIN

To appreciate the natural environment of California, you have to keep in mind the state's size and topography. On the one hand, Death Valley has some of the driest and hottest conditions on earth. On the other hand, coastal areas and snow-capped mountains contrast dramatically with such harsh desert conditions. One person hears the word "California" and thinks of majestic redwood trees, another envisions Santa Monica beach culture, another calls to mind the agricultural production of the state's central region, and yet another imagines only Hollywood. But it's naive and inaccurate to see California in such simple terms.

Up to this point, the biblical picture before us has been one dimensional: sin is to be forsaken and Christlike purity is to be practiced; believers are called to follow in the steps of Jesus and lead holy lives. But there's more to see in the Bible's textured landscape of spiritual life—in particular, some dark valleys. Texts spotlighting the pristine wonders of godliness need to be seen in tandem with other passages that probe into our depravity.

"Forgive Us Our Debts"

These two dimensions come together within the Lord's Prayer itself. In the first half the emphasis is on lofty visions of the Father's transforming power—of "heaven on earth" (see chapter 2). But in part two of Jesus' model prayer the direction of the petitions turns away from high hopes toward the pressures of discipleship here and now. The tone shifts as we appeal for "daily bread," forgiveness, and the Lord's leading away from temptation and the clutches of the Evil One, who's eager to bring believers into spiritual devastation through sin.

It's crucial to see how dramatic this change of perspective is. If the first part provides the scenic overlook, the second part has us down in the trenches where Jesus is brutally realistic about life's trials. Disciples have incurred debts—spiritual debts. We've sinned against the Lord, and there's a penalty for this. Further, we owe so much that we could never repay. But Jesus holds out hope when he instructs us to pray for forgiveness of our spiritual debts.

But how can we need forgiveness in a heavenlike life? To pray for forgiveness is implicitly to confess sin. And to acknowledge our future sin: we acknowledge we'll still be sinners tomorrow, and the next day, and so on, when we utter these necessary daily petitions. But how can we experience God's will and reign in heavenlike ways yet still sin on an ongoing basis? Solutions for this puzzle will emerge as we move forward in this study, but for now it's important to pursue the true dimensions of the believer's sin problem.

Jesus links our ongoing need of forgiveness with our ongoing practice of forgiveness: "Forgive us our debts, as we also have forgiven our debtors." Even as we plead with God to renew his pardon to us, we must (and ultimately will—if we belong to Christ) also extend forgiveness to others. By contrast, a life simply given over to the grudge reveals a soul unacquainted with God's forgiveness (Matthew 6:14–15). Not that true believers always do this immediately and flawlessly; we certainly have room for progress in following Jesus' lead (Colossians 3:13). But when a person receives mercy from the Lord, this stunning reality generates a joyful gratitude to God that overflows in the extending of grace toward others.

Our daily struggles also include "temptation"—the enticement to sin. Jesus instructs his followers to plead with the Father for protection from temptation. This isn't an appeal to somehow avoid encountering it. God doesn't offer the option of such an insulated life. Rather, it's a cry to be kept from falling headlong into sin. Temptation comes at us all day, every day. And not just to commit obvious sins such as stealing, lying, or greed (*I want that car*), but also more subtle ones such as being self-centered, discontent, downcast, or talking about others behind their backs. In the face of such grave danger, we're called to cling to the Father and plead for his deliverance. So we pray not only for forgiveness of past offenses, but also for protection from future sin traps and the Enemy's assaults.

"If We Confess Our Sins"

If the Lord's Prayer implies that Christians continue to sin, 1 John 1:8–10 states this fact plainly: "If we say we have no sin, we deceive ourselves, and the truth is not in us. If we confess our sins, he is faithful and just to forgive us our sins and to cleanse us from all unrighteousness. If we say we have not sinned, we make him a liar, and his word is not in us." It's especially important here to pick up that our sin problem extends into ongoing present time. Not only must believers admit they *have sinned*,[1] but also that they *have sin*. Christians simply aren't facing reality if they claim they no longer commit sin.

Bear in mind that John writes to Christian readers; this isn't an evangelistic letter, but a guide for sometimes-maturing, sometimes-floundering followers of Jesus who need guidance and encouragement. The readers are "children of God," John's spiritual "children," and

---

1. John's opponents who said they hadn't sinned (1 John 1:10) were not claiming they'd never sinned as unbelievers, but instead they denied sinning since coming to believe in Jesus Christ (so Thomas Schreiner, "Persevering in Faith Is Not Perfection," http://www.oakhill.ac.uk/downloads/audio/schreiner/mp3s/schreiner_2.mp3). The error of v. 8 is equivalent to the error of v. 10, despite the change of verb tense.

people whose sins have been forgiven. After reminding these believers in 1 John 1:1–4 of the rock-solid fact of Jesus' bodily resurrection, the first matter John turns to is walking in the light in a way that deals directly with ongoing sin.

Verses 6, 8, and 10 all begin with "If we claim . . ." (NIV). What do we claim—what do we *say* is true of our spiritual lives? Do we just talk the talk, or do we walk the talk as well? Do you claim to be following Jesus while slipping off into the darkness (e.g., by scanning the Internet for quick thrills, or joining the popular crowd that puts others down, or giving only stingy gifts to the work of Christ)? Are you putting up a good front? If we *claim* to be followers of Christ yet go on in the darkness, we are liars (v. 6) and our tall talk is worthless.

Christ-followers, of course, are without sin in the sense of sin's guilt charged against them—such guilt is cleared through justification. But still, we can't claim the practice of sin is just a thing of the past. First John 1:8 proves otherwise: we're spiritually "in process." Or to put it differently, our lives today are intertwined between the "now" and "not yet" of God's reign. John's thrust, then, is that believers need to face up to sin, including ongoing sin, and eagerly run back to the Father for forgiveness as they recognize their wayward conduct (1:9).

In very next sentence (2:1) John strikes with surprise, "My little children, I am writing these things to you so that you may not sin." John has told us we do sin, yet he writes so that we may not sin. Is he talking out of two sides of his mouth? In light of the rugged realities of human imperfection, is he slipping into a hopeless idealism? I think not. John takes a long-term view here—like looking down the road miles and miles ahead, toward a far-off destination on the horizon. And yet it's a vision that can be realized to some degree, and increasingly, in today's spiritual formation process. We may not be able to eradicate sin from our hearts this side of heaven, but by God's help we can take real steps toward Christlike holiness and love.

John goes on to say, "But if anyone does sin . . ." Idealism is balanced with realism; God's kingdom now is paired with his reign that's yet to be. The Lord's desire is that we would not sin, but he makes provision for the times when we do sin. As our "advocate," Jesus Christ steps up to the divine bench and speaks to the Father in our defense: "I know they committed high treason, but I took the full punishment and paid the full penalty for their crimes. So justice cannot condemn them. They go free." In fact, 1 John 2:2 presents Jesus as "the propitiation" for sin to placate the righteous wrath of the Father against rebel creatures. So, our gracious yet realistic God provides a way to experience his ongoing forgiveness even as he summons us to walk in the steps of Jesus, his Son (2:6).

The Christian's Identity

In his book *Birthright: Christian, Do You Know Who You Are?* David Needham argues that with conversion to Jesus Christ one not only receives forgiveness of sins, but also begins a life of an entirely new order, a life of God's presence within. He laments the way so many professing believers view themselves negatively: the "man in the mirror" is simply a forgiven sinner, and his life verse is 1 John 1:9. Believers who set their sights so low make very little positive impact in the world and often give up on the Christian life. The key problem is the failure of Christians to understand who they truly are: recipients of God's supernatural new creation, people truly alive for the first time who can experience a quality of life like the one Jesus experienced on this earth.

In the course of striving to lift Christians' sights above the dismal horizon of defeat and discouragement, Needham (following the NRSV) calls attention to certain passages in 1 John that have been associated with a teaching of Christian perfection:

- "If we say that we have fellowship with him while we are walking in darkness, we lie and do not do what is true; but if we walk in the light as he himself is in the light, we have fellowship with one another, and the blood of Jesus his Son cleanses us from all sin" (1:6–7).
- "My little children, I am writing these things to you so

that you may not sin. But if anyone does sin, we have an advocate with the Father, Jesus Christ the righteous" (2:1).

- "Whoever says, 'I abide in him,' ought to walk just as he walked" (2:6).
- "No one who abides in him sins; no one who sins has either seen him or known him" (3:6).
- "Those who have been born of God do not sin, because God's seed abides in them; they cannot sin, because they have been born of God" (3:9; see also 5:18).

What does John mean in 3:9 by "cannot sin"? Needham contends, "When John used the word *cannot*, I believe he was trying to communicate a critical point. Sinning . . . is so utterly irrational—so stupid—*no one in their right mind would ever consider sinning a reasonable behavior*."[2] "John considered the miracle of being born of God so radical, it produced a person who was truly righteous."[3] What's more, the force of 2:1 is not to excuse sin but to hold out the hope of living without sin. The conditional statement "If anybody does sin . . ." implies that sinful conduct is not normal or necessary, so it's possible not to sin.

Needham depicts various attempts to soften the sharp statements in these verses as feeble and misguided.[4] Further, he caricatures the position of those who don't believe the Scriptures hold out the possibility of sinless perfection as follows: "Sin is normal for the Christian life."[5] Unfortunately, this oversimplifies the alternatives to his conclusion, thus setting up opposing interpretations as straw men.[6] The truth is

---

2. Needham, *Birthright: Christian, Do You Know Who You Are?* Rev. ed. (Sisters, OR: Multnomah, 1999), 87 (emphasis in original).
3. Ibid., 88.
4. Ibid., 115.
5. Ibid., 116.
6. Instances of Needham knocking down "straw men" appear, e.g., on 65, 89, 109, 116, 120, 127–28, and 201.

that disagreeing with Needham doesn't obligate one to say, "Sin is normal for the Christian life."

The texts in 1 John, which Needham cites from the NRSV, seem to describe the Christian's departure from sin in absolute terms. As was noted in the previous chapter, however, the ESV renders the Greek present-tense verbs in 3:6; 3:9; and 5:18 in such a way as to encompass continuing action:

- "No one who abides in him keeps on sinning; no one who keeps on sinning has either seen him or known him" (3:6).
- "No one born of God makes a practice of sinning, for God's seed abides in him, and he cannot keep on sinning because he has been born of God" (3:9).
- "We know that everyone who has been born of God does not keep on sinning" (5:18).

The sense conveyed, then, is that habitually yielding to sin, or a lifestyle characterized by sin, is not possible for a person born of God and indwelt by the Holy Spirit.[7]

Needham considers the idea that a Christian would not habitually sin a "halfway solution" and actually "no solution at all."[8] But this is to assume what must be proved; a prohibition of habitual or ongoing ways of sin is only a poor (i.e., "halfway") solution if the biblical texts specify something else. Needham, however, doesn't explore the nuances of the Greek present tense to search out the possibility of continuing action in 3:6; 3:9; and 5:18. What's more, he doesn't acknowledge the fact that many who reject a perfectionist reading of 1 John attempt a legitimate undertaking by seeking to reconcile 1 John's "tall order" texts with those that assume (2:1; 5:16–17) or state (1:8–10) that believers practice sin. The challenge of developing a coherent theological understanding of sin and sanctification in 1 John requires such a "big picture" endeavor, yet Needham does not seriously attempt this task.

---

7. John Piper, *Finally Alive*, 147.
8. Needham, *Birthright*, 118–19.

The portrayal of God in the letters of John, then, is one that mixes and intermingles awesome holiness and bountiful grace. And in light of this richness of God's character, the message of 1 John is one that both upholds the beautiful ideal of Christlike conduct that turns away from sin, yet also reassures believers of the Lord's patient, generous offer of ongoing forgiveness and love. This delicate balance is akin to what we find in the Lord's Prayer: our yearning for "heaven on earth" stands in tension with a readiness to confess sin and call out for spiritual protection.

"We All Stumble in Many Ways"

I grew up in Minnesota so I have many memories from cold winter days, including playing broomball. Broomball is an odd twist on ice hockey—instead of a stick and a puck you use a broom to hit a ball (anywhere from the size of a softball to a volleyball, in my experience) into the goal. And you play the game in shoes, not skates. Being on ice with no blades is a great equalizer—fast runners and great athletes are humbled by the absence of traction and the constant risk of tailbone injuries. To be sure, with time and practice you learn some tricks to get better movement (like hovering along the edge of the rink and pushing off the boards at the right moment). But you never get past the place of instability and vulnerability. Tumbles may happen at any moment. It's part of normal broomball experience.

God's Word suggests there's also an ongoing hazard of stumbling spiritually. The Letter of James, for example, speaks directly about believers' continuing sin. In the context of teaching how all believers commit sins of speech, 3:2 generalizes: "We all stumble in many ways." What should believers do about the wide-ranging sins they trip into? James anticipates the question in 5:16: "Therefore, confess your sins to one another and pray for one another, that you may be healed." This admonition, of course, implies that believers have sins to confess.

If we widen our lens, various additional texts in the Old and New Testaments show that believers aren't only former sinners but also disciples who continue to stray. Jeremiah's analysis is apt: "The heart is deceitful above all things, and desperately sick; who can understand it?" (17:9). We'd like to say that such devious ways have been locked away in our unregenerate past, but the biblical portrayal would make that mere wishful thinking. We're "prone to wander," as the hymn writer Robert Robinson so aptly put it.[9]

The Psalms include various appeals for God's forgiveness. Best known is Psalm 51, in which David, a man who had long known the Lord, finally admits his vile sin and pours out his heart with contrition. "For I know my transgressions, and my sin is ever before me. Against you, you only, have I sinned and done what is evil in your sight, so that you may be justified in your words and blameless in your judgment" (51:3–4). The stain of sin torments David as he falls down before the Holy One, and he cries out, "Create in me a clean heart, O God, and renew a right spirit within me" (v. 10).[10]

It's similar with the New Testament. Jesus' assessment of his disciples in the hour of trial is apt: "The spirit indeed is willing, but the flesh is weak" (Mark 14:38). Those who come to Christ find themselves identifying with the desperate father who asks Jesus to rescue his demon-possessed son: "I believe; help my unbelief!" (Mark 9:24). So the situation is complex; it's not just a matter of believing or not, or intending to do the right thing or not. The life of faith is a conflicted experience when it comes to the indwelling sin and the pursuit of godliness.

"Wretched Man That I Am"

The most prominent biblical text about the conflicted soul in turmoil over sin is Romans 7:14–25. For John Owen, this passage was so pivotal for understanding the believer's indwelling sin that he made it the backbone of his major writings on the topic.[11] "For we know that

---

9. Robert Robinson, "Come, Thou Fount of Every Blessing" (1758).
10. See also Psalms 32:3–5; 85:4–6; 139:23–24.
11. John Owen, *Sin and Temptation: The Challenge to Personal Godliness*, Classics of

the law is spiritual, but I am of the flesh, sold under sin. For I do not understand my own actions. For I do not do what I want, but I do the very thing I hate." In his "inner being" Paul delights to follow God's law, but he also complains that there is another law waging war against him that would take him captive to the "law of sin." "Wretched man that I am! Who will deliver me from this body of death? Thanks be to God through Jesus Christ our Lord! So then, I myself serve the law of God with my mind, but with my flesh I serve the law of sin."

This intense spiritual struggle is presented by Paul in the first person and present tense, so it's understandable that many have assumed he's speaking of his own Christian experience, and that Romans 7, in bold and candid fashion, reveals the battle against sin that's inherent to authentic Christian experience. Further, it's the battle of an exemplary apostle many years after his conversion, so we can't brush the text aside as the unfortunate struggle of an immature believer.

In recent decades, however, another perspective on this passage has gained attention, namely the view that the "I" is not specifically Paul the Christian but rather his pre-Christian self now seen with hindsight from the standpoint of belief. The present tense makes the struggle vivid, but it portrays a wrestling match with the law that would characterize a zealous Jew and not a justified Jewish Christian like Paul. This interpretation gains support from Romans 6:14 ("sin will have no dominion over you"); 6:18 and 22 (the Christian has been "set free from sin"); and 8:2 (believers have been set free in Christ from the law of sin and death). Paul speaks of his freedom in Christ, presenting himself in terms that seem incompatible with the "carnal" person of 7:14.[12]

Faith and Devotion, James M. Houston, ed. (Portland: Multnomah, 1983), e.g., 4, 20, 28, 133.

12. See, e.g., Douglas Moo's commentary (*Romans* [NICNT, n.s.; Grand Rapids: Eerdmans, 1996], 441–51) for a survey of the issues and relevant literature, a helpful discussion of key questions, and a plausible argument that Romans 7:14–25 does not refer to Christian experience.

I have two thoughts about this alternative reading of Romans 7. First, I don't find it persuasive. Granted, interpreting the passage is difficult; there are factors that seem to lean in various directions. But the historic reading of the text as describing the Christian's struggle with sin makes best sense of the first-person singular pronouns and the present tense (notice the shift away from past time after 7:13). Further, the present age is portrayed as a time of "groaning"—not only creation, but "we ourselves" (8:23) groan as we await the completion of our adoption and redemption.[13] Moreover, the sequence of Paul's cry of relief and gratitude in 7:25a ("Thanks be to God through Jesus Christ our Lord!") followed by 7:25b ("So then, I myself serve the law of God with my mind, but with my flesh I serve the law of sin") is awkward and anticlimactic if the turmoil of 7:14–25 is that of an unbeliever. I've benefited from J. I. Packer's overview and analysis, in which he argues that the "I" in this text is indeed Paul the believer and thus, by inference, every Christian.[14]

But second, since the matter is so hotly contested in New Testament scholarship, we won't focus attention on Romans 7. This, however, won't keep us from forming a comprehensive, consistent biblical basis for the life of spiritual formation regarding the interplay of indwelling sin and progressive sanctification. The message of Romans 7 would add depth and color to the message, but it wouldn't alter its substance. So it's to that wider pursuit that we return.

Modeling the Life of Faith

In addition to texts stating or implying that Christians continue to sin after coming to faith in Christ, the Bible presents numerous examples of believers, including some of the most exemplary heroes of faith,

---

13. James D. G. Dunn, *Romans* (WBC 38A, 38B; Waco, TX: Word, 1988), 1.387–89, 403–12.
14. E.g., J. I. Packer, "The 'Wretched Man' Revisited: Another Look at Romans 7:14–25," 70–81 in Sven K. Soderlund and N. T. Wright, eds., *Romans and the People of God: Essays in Honor of Gordon D. Fee on the Occasion of His 65th Birthday* (Grand Rapids: Eerdmans, 1999), 70–81.

who stumble and falter in their walk with God. These texts "say" by their consistent portrayal that true believers continue to wrestle with sin.

The apostle Peter, although recognized as leader among the disciples (Matthew 16:16–19; Luke 22:31–32), manages to stumble again and again. He presumptuously tries to block Jesus from going to the cross, for which he's soundly rebuked: "Get behind me, Satan!" (Matthew 16:23). Though he dares to step on the sea to go to Jesus, his faith falters and he sinks (Matthew 14:28–31). Peter sleeps on the Mount of Transfiguration and ends up, once awake, uttering nonsense in a bumbling attempt to bottle the moment of glory (Luke 9:33). In the end, in a self-serving way he denies even knowing Jesus (Matthew 26:69–75).

Andrew Murray, however, suggests that such failings vanish from Peter's life after Pentecost and the coming of the Spirit. His denial of Jesus and response of bitter weeping (Luke 22:61–62) formed "the turning-point in the history of Peter." As a result, he was changed: "Peter was a man of absolute surrender; he gave up all to follow Jesus. . . . Peter's whole nature was changed. The work that Christ began in Peter when He looked upon him, was perfected when he was filled with the Holy Ghost." Murray goes on: "Dear friend, I beseech you, look at Peter utterly changed—the self-pleasing, the self-trusting, the self-seeking Peter, full of sin, continually getting into trouble, foolish and impetuous, but now filled with the Spirit and the life of Jesus."[15]

But Murray is strangely silent about Peter's hypocrisy noted in Galatians 2:11–14, in which Paul takes Peter to task for retreating from table fellowship with Gentile Christians when leaders from the Jerusalem church came to see them in Antioch. Peter goes back on his own convictions (cf. Acts 15:11) by treating Gentile believers as second-class spiritual citizens. This is no small failing. And it implies

---

15. Andrew Murray, *Absolute Surrender* (http://www.ccel.org/ccel/murray/surrender.html). See chap. 4, "Peter's Repentance."

that, despite certain advances in faith and ministry, Peter grappled with sin and temptation all his days.[16]

So too, other disciples act sinfully, for example, by clutching at greatness (Mark 10:35–45) or fleeing from Christ in the time of trial (Mark 14:50). In addition, sin problems in various New Testament churches are painfully evident (consider the church at Corinth with its array of sins and eccentricities or the various churches of Asia Minor addressed in Revelation 2–3). Similarly, Paul asserts that he's not yet perfect (Philippians 3:12, i.e., not yet fully mature in Christ—he hasn't "arrived"); in fact, he's the chief of sinners (see 1 Timothy 1:15 KJV).

John Wesley notes Paul's declaration in Philippians 3:12 in *A Plain Account of Christian Perfection*,[17] yet he goes on to describe the "perfect Christian" in a rich variety of absolute terms: "He is therefore happy in God; yea, always happy, as having in him a well of water springing up unto everlasting life, and over-flowing his soul with peace and joy." This Christian prays without ceasing, his heart is always lifted up to God, the Lord is in all his thoughts, and he walks with God continually. "All the talents he has, he constantly employs according to his Master's will; every power and faculty of his soul, every member of his body." In all he does he not only aims at God's glory, "but actually attains it; his business and his refreshments, as well as his prayers, all serve to this great end. . . . Nor do the customs of the world at all hinder his 'running the race which is set before him.'" He *cannot* lay up treasures on earth, speak evil of a neighbor, or utter an unkind word; no corrupt conversation ever comes out of his mouth. In the end, however, Wesley's perfectionist description clashes with the Bible's portrayal, and it invites false expectations of a

---

16. We should not miss how this fact lends credibility to the Bible as the unvarnished Word of God telling the tale of spiritual transformation with brazen honesty.

17. John Wesley, *A Plain Account of Christian Perfection* (http://www.ccel.org/ccel/wesley/perfection/files/perfection.html), sec. 10. Wesley's bold statement that "the kingdom of heaven is now set up on earth" (sec. 12) lacks a balancing awareness of the future dimensions of God's reign.

uniformly victorious life here and now. That, in turn, can lead to all kinds of confusion and discouragement.[18] By contrast, in the first of his Ninety-five Theses Martin Luther shows a biblical realism: "When our Lord and Master, Jesus Christ, said 'Repent,' He called for the entire life of believers to be one of repentance."[19]

The biblical portrait of Mary and Martha provides a helpful case study (John 11). You could say Mary and Martha live with the dissonance of honest discipleship: they love and trust Jesus, yet they also get caught up in self-centered thinking. Grief is heavy in the air—Mary and Martha's brother Lazarus has died, relatives are wailing, tears are flowing—it's too much to bear. When the sisters learn that Jesus is finally coming to see them, a surviving shred of faith tumbles out in their declaration that he could have healed Lazarus. They assume this about no one else who visits their home. It reveals faith and comes from the heart.

But still, they wrongly assume Jesus would have healed their brother if only he hadn't been so far away or had come on time. So you could say they believe in Jesus, but only to a point: they trust him as long as he makes things go the way *they* think they should go. Sudden suffering jars these genuine disciples into saying that, in effect, their Lord doesn't measure up—that circumstances have overwhelmed Jesus and that he's failed them. It doesn't dawn on them that Jesus' late arrival is purposeful and even good.

Mary and Martha exhibit a flawed yet genuine devotion to Jesus. Their allegiance is tainted by fear, false assumptions, and attempts to deny his lordship. Still, the Master loves these imperfect sisters. Although he corrects them and implicitly rebukes them for their fair-weather faith, he still very much feels for them and lifts them out of the dark pit of sorrow. Honest believers who are willing to see their

---

18. See Stephen Neill, *Christian Holiness* (New York: Harper, 1960), 36, for a thoughtful critique of perfectionist teachings.

19. Martin Luther, Ninety-five Theses (http://www.spurgeon.org/~phil/history/95theses.htm), thesis 1.

own reflection in mixed-up Martha and Mary can rest in the arms of a gracious Savior—one who truly orchestrates all things together for their good!

Characters in the Old Testament

If we widen the lens to include the Old Testament, again we see that authentic believers are flawed and unfinished: Adam and Eve are placed in Paradise, yet they rebel against the Lord and succumb to temptation. Noah, despite having found favor in the eyes of the Lord, wallows in drunkenness and sexual misconduct.[20] Despite Abraham's many upright and God-honoring deeds, twice he puts his wife in danger, lying and selfishly saying Sarah is his sister, thus making a mockery of God's covenant promise of descendants. Sarah may be a model of faith (Hebrews 11:11; 1 Peter 3:5–6), but she also laughs at the Lord's promises and lashes out at Hagar and Ishmael. Isaac follows in his father's steps and selfishly puts his wife in grave danger. Rebekah favors Jacob over Esau and connives with Jacob to deceive Isaac. Jacob manipulates and deceives Esau, and later he also shows favoritism to one of his children, Joseph. And that's just in Genesis!

Although Moses is a great leader and demonstrates faith in many ways (Hebrews 11:23–29; cf. 3:2), he commits murder, resists the Lord's leading in his life, and in an outburst of temper disobeys God. Brave Gideon falls into idolatry, and mighty Samson is swept away by lust and sexual sin. David, the man after God's own heart, is infamous for committing lust, adultery, and murder. Solomon may have great wisdom, but he's eventually swayed by foreign wives to go after their gods. Hezekiah trusts God for protection from Assyrian invaders, but later in life he looks instead to human powers for security. Job may be blameless and upright, fearing God and turning away from evil,[21]

---

20. Bruce Demarest, *The Cross and Salvation* (Foundations of Evangelical Theology; Wheaton: Crossway, 1997), 416.
21. Job 1:1, 8, 22; 2:10. Demarest clarifies that the term "blameless" (*tāmîm*) in Ps. 15:2 indicates "not sinless perfection but moral soundness, uprightness, and integrity"

but through his great calamity he discovers deep-seated sin in his own heart and so repents "in dust and ashes." Isaiah the prophet sees his sin vividly when coming before the Holy One of Israel, crying out, "Woe is me!" Daniel, despite his spiritual vigilance in the den of lions, includes his own sins in a prayer of corporate confession. The prophet Micah doesn't hesitate to admit his sin before God.

This long list of very imperfect believers we meet in the biblical narrative begs for an answer to the question, Why is it that, if God is telling us not to sin but to be obedient and lead holy lives, the believers we meet in the pages of the Bible do not measure up? Why is it that, instead, they exhibit ongoing failings in sin even as they aspire to walk (and sometimes make real progress in walking) in faith and obedience? This leads us to a key dilemma of this study. On the one hand, it seems that the Lord expects his people to conduct themselves in a holy manner. On the other hand, the Scriptures recognize that God's people continue to be sinners and do not experience *in this life* the unmixed, thoroughgoing holiness that is urged upon them. How do we reconcile these biblical motifs? We begin to respond to such questions in chapter 4.

(ibid., 417). It is fitting, in light of Job 42:5–6, to understand "blameless" (*tom*) in Job 1:1 in a similar manner. Consider also the mingling of David's confession of sin and appeal to his own "integrity" (*tom*) in Ps. 41:4, 12.

FIGHTING BACK:
WAGING SPIRITUAL WARFARE

On a sunny day in late October the steep slopes surrounding the Pocono Mountain town of Jim Thorpe almost look like they're on fire, so brilliant are the autumn leaves. Pennsylvania boasts some truly spectacular scenery, thanks to crimson fire-bush leaves, bright yellow maples, and so many other kinds of foliage. And yet it's an ever-changing landscape. The long shadows of winter's darker days color most everything in shades of brown and gray, though the occasional snowfall brightens things up. And then, eventually, radiant magnolia and dogwood blossoms light up the spring horizon with new life. Soon after that, leaves burst on the scene, and the world is green all over again. The cycle of seasons hints at the breadth of God's creative ingenuity.

And so, a Jim Thorpe tourist in February (perhaps visiting nearby ski resorts) will come away with a very different impression than the autumn visitor, thanks to the colors, temperatures, and moods of the various seasons. If you insist that Jim Thorpe means red and yellow trees, you're not seeing the whole truth, so too, if you envision only a deep green carpet spreading over the rolling Pocono hills. The reality is just too "big" to be contained in a simplistic description.

Likewise, the reality of the Christian life is simply too complex to fit into a simple summary challenge such as "Be holy" *or* "Confess your sins." A basic idea of the Christian as *either* an upright saint *or* a forgiven sinner misrepresents the multifaceted truth. We won't develop a full and fair biblical picture of authentic spiritual life until we view it in all "seasons." The preceding chapters have provided two crucial perspectives, namely, the lofty vision of Christlike godliness and the lowly reality of laboring with ongoing sin. Both pictures are correct—that is, both accurately present the Christian life as seen from certain angles.

Our purpose here is to search the Scriptures for helpful ways to understand how these two realities—holiness and sin—intermingle in Bible-based churches and Christian lives. And what we see is that the movement from sinful toward godly living involves *effort*.[1] Among the Bible's images conveying this idea are these three: waging war, doing work, and engaging in athletic competition. By exploring passages under these headings, we'll become better equipped to make sense of the contrast between Christians as sinners and as saints.

Mixing Metaphors

In Paul's final letter to young Pastor Timothy, he combines all three images:

---

1. At the same time, it's fitting to clarify that the biblical commendation of effort and "good works" always grounds such human activity in divine grace and enablement. "We love because he first loved us" (1 John 4:19). Work out your own salvation, for God is at work within you (Phil. 2:12–13). Justification by faith and not works is a core concept rooted in the Old Testament (e.g., Gen. 15:6; Hab. 2:4) and unpacked in various New Testament writings (e.g., Rom. 1:16–17; 4:3; Gal. 3:6, 11; Heb. 10:38–39; cf. James 2:23). Good deeds flow out from a heart of humble, thankful faith (so the "obedience of faith" in Rom. 1:5; 16:26; cf. Gal. 5:6).

> You then, my child, be strengthened by the grace that is in Christ Jesus, and what you have heard from me in the presence of many witnesses entrust to faithful men who will be able to teach others also. Share in suffering as a good *soldier* of Christ Jesus. No soldier gets entangled in civilian pursuits, since his aim is to please the one who enlisted him. An *athlete* is not crowned unless he competes according to the rules. It is the hard-working *farmer* who ought to have the first share of the crops. Think over what I say, for the Lord will give you understanding in everything. (2 Timothy 2:1–7, italics added)

Before offering these three analogies, Paul makes it clear in 2:1 that divine power provided graciously through Christ Jesus is foundational for the effort behind Christian conduct. The passive verb ("be strengthened") alludes to the working of God, as does the mention of "grace." Even though Timothy is urged to receive grace, strength remains a gift from the Lord. In light of Paul's emphasis elsewhere on powerful divine initiative in salvation and the Christian life,[2] this comes as no surprise here.

In this passage, Paul employs military language to portray the spiritual life—a life that includes "suffering." Of course, no informed soldier goes to war without realizing that injury and pain (or even death) may strike. Such conventional wisdom about war is beyond dispute, and yet when it's transferred figuratively to the Christian life, believers look up and take notice. "Suffering" may well not be what many have in mind as they dream of the "abundant life." Paul adds that soldiers don't get "entangled in civilian pursuits." Such distraction and diversion are completely out of character for the intense, life-and-death focus called for on the battlefield.

---

2. E.g., Rom. 8:28–30; Eph. 1:4–6; 2:8–10; Phil. 2:12–13.

He then shifts to athletic competition and the need to follow the rules in order to win. The obvious implication is that it's desirable to win. Who tries out to enter the Olympic Games without a deep longing to stand on the medal platform? The 2008 Beijing Summer Olympics drew attention to many athletic superstars, with the American swimmer Michael Phelps receiving as much visibility as anyone. In the course of winning eight gold medals, Phelps exhibited an obvious tenacity, a ferociously competitive spirit. Being the best of the best was his great ambition. Of course, Olympic officials watched every move and every turn in the pool to make sure the rules were followed; one departure from "the law" would mean disqualification. So too, the life of faith involves straining forward, stretching for the finish line, while competing within the parameters of God's will.

Then Paul changes the image to ordinary labor—farming, to be specific. A hardworking farmer deserves the first share of the crops; a lazy one, by implication, does not. Since the farmer's family needs to eat, it's a given that obtaining a share of the crops is good and right. As with the military and athletic illustrations, here too a key component is full-fledged effort. Further, these analogies aren't abstract ideas, but practical images of vigorous labor for the Lord. No matter how we resolve the tension between Christians as saints and as sinners, then, it's apparent already that twisting grace into sloth would be no solution at all.

Of course, numerous other texts of Scripture utilize images of warfare, work, and athletics to teach about authentic spiritual experience, and so we turn to each word-picture in order.

Spiritual Warfare

At the end of World War II, ticker-tape parades added an exclamation point to the relief Americans felt. Alfred Eisenstaedt's famous photo, "V-J Day in Times Square" (with sailor and nurse kissing), conveys this exuberance: *the war is over!* And yet, the notion of a neatly demarcated time frame with starting and ending points isn't so helpful when it comes to spiritual warfare (in this respect the "war on terror" may provide a better analogy). To be sure, the New Testament does anticipate a cessation of hostilities, but not this side of heaven. Life as we know it here and now is characterized by, and will always be characterized by, waging war against sin and Satan.[3] When there's victory on one front, breaches of security or unanticipated assaults take place on some other side. Even when major spiritual battles are won, the war rages on.

Accounts of warfare in the Old Testament are numerous, but their relevance for us is minimal. To be sure, the rescue of Lot in Genesis, the conquests in Canaan, Gideon's defeat of the Midianites in Judges, and David's contest with Goliath in 1 Samuel—to name just a few instances—have certain spiritual dimensions. That is, these accounts may feature a zeal for God's glory and dependence on divine provision, and as such they have some exemplary value for the Christian life of faith. But still, the act of literally waging war as narrated in the Old Testament framework is not, in and of itself, a model of any kind for the New Testament Christian.

To clarify this point, there are certain distinctions between the way God related to humanity prior to the coming of Messiah and the way he has operated since Christ entered the world. God's design for Israel was to be a "light for the nations" (Isaiah 42:6; 49:6); through Abraham the Lord would bless all peoples (Genesis 12:1–3). So it's never been God's plan to favor Israel and disregard other people groups. But still, in Old Testament times God's way of relating to the world was through his chosen people Israel, the centerpiece of his gracious work on earth. And within that time frame in the history of

---

3. The victory Paul speaks of in 2 Tim. 4:7 ("I have fought the good fight, I have finished the race") may be phrased as an outcome already realized, but that's only because he believes his life is over ("the time of my departure has come," 4:6).

salvation, the use of physical force was permitted and at times even commanded for the purpose of establishing and enhancing Israel (e.g., Joshua 8–11).

But with Christ's global Great Commission to make disciples among all the people groups on earth, a dramatic shift of approach was put into effect. If the Old Testament pattern was "come and see" (i.e., come and see the bright light of God's glory shining out from his people Israel), in the New Testament it is "go and tell." What's more, although the people of God in Old Testament times were united along national and ethnic lines, with Christ's coming and his missionary commission, the people of God have been reconstituted as a multiethnic, international fellowship spreading all over the earth and among all populations. The theocracy under which Old Testament Israel lived has been eclipsed by a different form of "government," the church, the worldwide suprapolitical fellowship of Christ-followers. And so, in light of this shift in God's *modus operandi*, we'll look beyond the warfare texts in the Old Testament.

Since the New Testament fellowship of Christ-followers isn't an army, and since the church is not beholden somehow to enforce the will of any nation-state, it comes as no surprise that the kind of warfare spoken of in the New Testament is spiritual in nature. To be sure, the notion of "enemy" is not eliminated, but the way enemies are to be viewed and treated is radically modified. Jesus teaches his disciples to love their human enemies. The only adversary Christians are to fight is Satan, drawing on spiritual weaponry. Therefore, I want to be clear that there is no New Testament basis for the church to marshal an army, exert military force, or coerce people in any way. To do so (e.g., as happened in the Crusades) would be to drastically and tragically misread the Bible and misconstrue the nature of the Christian life. What's more, the impact Christians seek as they love their neighbors and spread the good news is an impact made ultimately by God and God alone (1 Corinthians 3:6).[4]

If we focus on spiritual battle with Satan, then, a key place to turn is Jesus' temptation in the wilderness. Even though Satan maneuvered in unparalleled ways to tempt Jesus, and even though the experience of the Son of God in facing demonic enticement had aspects that were utterly unique, this account has crucial teaching value for today's Christian.

The Devil's tactic is to target anticipated weaknesses of Jesus, such as his natural hunger following forty days of fasting. Jesus is urged to draw on divine power to turn stones into bread. The Devil also tempts Jesus, presumably appealing to notions of ambition and pride, to create a spectacle of supernatural power and to gain earthly greatness and glory. Thus Satan targets what he believes are weaknesses, and it's reasonable to infer that he does the same when tempting any and every Christian.

Jesus' strategy in response to each temptation is to quote God's Word: "It is written . . . ." Of course, to draw on God's truth one must know it; if the sword of the Spirit is the Word of God (Ephesians 6:17), the believer must wear it in order to wield it. Christians must be immersed in the Scriptures and prepared to deploy them "on the battlefield." God's Word is intensely relevant to life's trials, including facing the Evil One's most insidious temptations. The Word of God is sharper than any two-edged sword—i.e., superior to earthly weapons—and it is sufficient for accomplishing deep spiritual heart work (Hebrews 4:12).

Ephesians 6:10–20 clarifies that there's more to withstanding the Devil's schemes than knowing biblical truths, crucial as this is. For example, putting on "the whole armor of God" involves the exercise of faith and the practice of prayer. The passage also links "salvation,"

---

4. And so, calling Archippus or Epaphroditus a "fellow soldier" (Philem. 2; Phil. 2:25) draws attention to their spiritual allegiance to Christ and his mission of love.

"righteousness," and "the gospel of peace" with the armor of God. These pieces of spiritual armor are unified by their focus on God's provision: faith and prayer center on the power of God; salvation, righteousness, and the gospel are gifts from the Lord. The proper soul stance for facing satanic opposition, then, is radical God reliance. Correspondingly, we're sure to fall in battle against the Evil One if we rely on our own power and wisdom.

God's goal for believers is to "stand"—to endure the Devil's attacks and persevere in faith. The tone of the text is optimistic, not unlike 1 Corinthians 10:13 (see chapter 2). Sincere believers should conclude that, to the degree they turn from sin and rely on God's armor and follow his sufficient Word amid the raging conflict with the Enemy, they can expect to stand firm. There is reason to be hopeful. God has given us the resources to advance in the battle with the Devil.

The fourth chapter of the book of James gives us this instruction: "Submit yourselves therefore to God. Resist the devil, and he will flee from you. Draw near to God, and he will draw near to you." The pattern is similar to Jesus' temptation and Ephesians 6, namely, that victory comes as we exercise trust in the Lord and firm resistance against Satan's ploys. It's a two-part movement, resisting the Devil *and* drawing near to God. This calls for a two-part passion: running far from sin and Satan and clinging closely to our strong and loving Lord.

Peter warns believers, "Be sober-minded; be watchful. Your adversary the devil prowls around like a roaring lion, seeking someone to devour. Resist him, firm in your faith" (1 Peter 5:8–9). The imagery of a prowling lion is unsettling; the Devil is not only vicious and powerful but crafty as well. Presumptuous believers who don't grapple with their very real vulnerability to satanic assault are in serious spiritual danger. Prevailing against the Enemy calls for deepest humility and reliance on God.

Faith is the strategic target of the Enemy's spiritual attacks—the roaring lion devours faith. A believer must plan to "fight the good fight *of faith*" (1 Timothy 6:12, italics added). The battle plan to overcome the world and gain spiritual victory is *faith* (1 John 5:4). Paul, knowing that the Thessalonian church had been under spiritual assault from "the tempter," longed to see if they stood firm: "For this reason, when I could bear it no longer, I sent to learn about your *faith*, for fear that somehow the tempter had tempted you and our labor would be in vain" (1 Thessalonians 3:5).

Since faith is the focus of the Enemy's spiritual attacks, it's vital for believers to wage war by reinforcing their trust in Christ. In this regard, Romans 10:17 brings the Word of God back to center stage: "So faith comes from hearing, and hearing through the word of Christ." Faith is generated (or renewed) as we receive the message of the Bible. God's Word is vital, then, not only as a weapon of attack but also for the personal heart fitness of the believer.

In 2 Corinthians Paul again uses military language in portraying the Christian life. First, the "weapons" of Christian spiritual warfare are *not* the weapons of the world. Military and political powers use various forms of coercion to bring others into submission to their will, ranging from every kind of violent uprising to all exertion of legitimate power under law. But spiritual warfare is another matter entirely. "For though we walk in the flesh, we are not waging war according to the flesh. For the weapons of our warfare are not of the flesh but have divine power to destroy strongholds" (2 Corinthians 10:3–4).

The ambiguity of the Christian life is expressed here in our relationship to "the flesh." On the one hand, believers are "in the flesh"; we lead embodied lives just like all our neighbors and are not immune to any earthly trials. At the same time, however, we're not "of the flesh," and our weapons of warfare as Christians aren't "fleshly"—they don't involve human force. We wage a different kind of war in which the ultimate enemy is not people—not even people who hate or hurt Christians—but Satan.

Further, the believer's triumph in spiritual battle is the Lord's work: "But thanks be to God, who in Christ always leads us in triumphal procession, and through us spreads the fragrance of the knowledge of him everywhere" (2 Corinthians 2:14). God's victory is centered in the life, death, and resurrection of Christ, so it's through our attachment to Christ that we're led in "triumphal procession." This imagery conveys the ancient custom of military heroes parading captured enemy soldiers through city streets in order to flaunt their conquest and heap scorn on their foes (cf. Colossians 2:15). The twist on this historical background here, however, is that it's the believer who's led by the conquering Christ—a benevolent procession led by the victorious King, and one that draws attention to the defeat of our sin and guilt through his great conquest.

The New Testament urges Christians not only to wage war against Satan, but also to slay their own sinful practices: "For if you live according to the flesh you will die, but if by the Spirit you put to death the deeds of the body, you will live" (Romans 8:13). This spiritual death sentence is focused on the church—each pronoun ("you") in the Greek text is plural. In other words, God isn't just urging believing individuals to execute sins they see in their own hearts and lives. Rather, fellowships of Christians are also to hunt down and kill sins that lurk within their communal lives. Similarly, Colossians 3:5 underscores the need of believers to patrol their corporate experience for ongoing sin: "Put to death therefore what is earthly in you: sexual immorality, impurity, passion, evil desire, and covetousness, which is idolatry."

The call to "mortify" sin, to put it to death, emphasizes the seriousness of the problem. It won't suffice to "manage" or "contain" sin or "make a truce" with it. We're called to make a determined spiritual assault, fighting "to the death." And yet, the analogy of killing breaks down at a point. There's a finality about literal killing, but sin doesn't "stay dead." Slaying our transgressions is a lifelong assault.

John Owen underscores the ongoing nature of mortification: "Never think of sin or lust as dead because it lies dormant."[5] Accordingly, the actual aim in this act of "killing" is to gain ground against our habits of sin. And yet, Owen also echoes the unqualified biblical call to practice holiness and exterminate sin: "Since the very nature of sin is enmity, the only relief one can find is to utterly destroy it."[6] "Without obedience to all of God's Word and all of God's provisions for salvation, isolated acts of mortification avail little. Universal obedience is essential."[7] This illustrates a lingering tension within Owen's writings, and yet it seems to be a reproduction of the basic biblical paradox before us: believers are called to practice holiness (i.e., stop sinning) yet also to confess sin and wage war against it (because the battle is ongoing).

Jesus' summons to cross bearing is also a call to kill. "And he said to all, 'If anyone would come after me, let him deny himself and take up his cross daily and follow me'" (Luke 9:23). Crucifixion was a form of capital punishment used by the Romans especially for the most despicable offenders; it not only inflicted lingering misery but also imposed ultimate shame. Strictly speaking, this isn't a warfare image. But like mortification, cross bearing is an act of "spiritual violence"— brute soul force applied in combat against the impulses of our sin. The inclusion of "daily" in Luke 9:23 helps clarify that the clash with sin and the process of putting the sin nature to death are ongoing.

Owen clarifies that, ultimately, only the Spirit of God can mortify sin.[8] Human exertion is a God-appointed means, but sin is put to death "by the Spirit" (Romans 8:13). Similarly, Ephesians 6:10–20

---

5. John Owen, *Sin and Temptation*, 158; see also 67, 152, 154, 156, 160.
6. Ibid., 16.
7. Ibid., 166.
8. Ibid., 90, 153.

teaches that God's provision is necessary to withstand the Devil's schemes (it's the "armor *of God*") and that prevailing in spiritual battle involves prayer that depends on God's power.

Toiling against Sin

From images of warfare we turn to biblical texts about toil and labor in opposition to sin. From this angle, as well, we see that a life of active faith in God involves hard work. And, surprisingly, such exertion includes contending with God himself. For example, a heart of concern for the people of Sodom moves Abraham to labor in prayer, pleading with the Lord to relent from his threatened judgment if righteous people can still be found there (Genesis 18:22–33; cf. Exodus 32:30–33). Jacob wrestles with God through the night, crying out to receive a blessing (Genesis 32:22–32). Nehemiah weeps, fasts, and mourns for days, contending with God in prayer on behalf of the Holy City with its walls in ruins (Nehemiah 1:1–11).

Job, as he grieves the loss of his children and scrapes his wretched sores, mounts a sustained series of objections to and challenges against the Lord. The speeches of his friends play a part, but the "main event" in the book of Job is the righteous man's struggle with his God. And, of course, numerous psalms give voice to spiritual toil, laboring in prayer, and pleading with God for power, protection, and mercy (e.g., Psalms 3, 6, 7, 10, 13, 22, and many more). Jeremiah struggles with the Lord amid the various hardships he must endure as he delivers warnings of judgment.[9] He announces that the people will seek and find the Lord God when they labor wholeheartedly to find him (Jeremiah 29:13). The prophet Habakkuk contends with the Almighty in cycles of prayer after learning that God would use the more wicked to punish the less wicked.

---

9. E.g., being placed in stocks (Jer. 20:1–7), imprisoned and beaten (37:11–15), and assigned a life of singleness to symbolize the demise of the coming generation (16:1–18).

Jesus commends a lifestyle of prayerful "wrestling" with God: ask, seek, knock (Matthew 7:7–11); seek first the kingdom of God (6:33). Further, Jesus teaches his disciples to emulate the persistent friend who comes at midnight (Luke 11:5–8) and the relentless widow (Luke 18:1–8) by persevering in prayer. And yet, even though the human spirit may be willing to follow the Lord, this task is very difficult since "the flesh is weak" (Mark 14:38). The work of contending with God through prayer is hard.

Horizontal labor is also crucial. Paul's Corinthian correspondence is a picture of spiritual toil "in the trenches" of teaching, correcting, and striving to overcome opponents of the gospel that threaten the church. Paul and Timothy, after enduring grave afflictions in the work of ministry, call on the Corinthians to help them through prayer (2 Corinthians 1:8–11). To the Colossians Paul writes, "For I want you to know how great a struggle I have for you and for those at Laodicea and for all who have not seen me face to face, that their hearts may be encouraged" (Colossians 2:1–2). He toils and strives to see Timothy trained in godliness (1 Timothy 4:7–10)—of course, this involves dependence on God's power. The outworking of such efforts would include Timothy's labor as an approved worker who rightly handles the Word of Truth (2 Timothy 2:15).

A unique angle on the effort of Christian living is the analogy of labor pains. Opponents of Paul's ministry at Galatia sought to draw people's allegiance away from him and toward themselves. At root, the Galatians were wavering in their commitment to the gospel. Paul mingles affection and dismay as he reflects on this problem: "My little children, for whom I am again in the anguish of childbirth until Christ is formed in you!" (Galatians 4:19). It's laborious for the apostle to lead these believers through the difficult process of spiritual formation.

Creation in general is in labor, but this cosmic struggle manifests itself in believers' lives as well: "For we know that the whole creation has been groaning together in the pains of childbirth until now. And not only the creation, but we ourselves, who have the firstfruits of the Spirit, groan inwardly as we wait eagerly for adoption as sons, the redemption of our bodies" (Romans 8:22–23). Thus the present-age experience of Christians is one of struggle and toil. We have the "firstfruits of the Spirit" (cf. 1 Corinthians 15:23), the initial installment of final glorification, and yet the era of spiritual labor still goes on. Naturally, because God's saving work (e.g., adoption, redemption) *will* be accomplished, ours is a hopeful "groaning."

Training for Athletic Competition

In addition to warfare and work, the Bible portrays Christian living through athletic imagery. Such passages strongly imply that following Christ is a vigorous undertaking that engages a person's whole being. Why do athletes endure the rigors of serious training? Because they have a passion to win. Just so, no follower of Jesus rightly understands the life of discipleship apart from a rightful longing to gain a glorious prize. But what is the prize, and how do believers compete for it?

Usain Bolt of Jamaica claimed track and field's center stage at the 2008 Olympics, taking gold and setting world records in the 100- and 200-meter sprints. With a voracious drive to be the best, in 2009 he extended his dominance and set even faster world records for both events at the World Championships in Berlin: 9.58 seconds in the 100 and 19.19 in the 200. In fact, at Berlin he took more than a tenth of a second off his 2008 record time, and that's the largest margin of improvement in the 100-meter world record since electronic timing became mandatory in 1977.[10] And Bolt won the 200 at Berlin by the largest margin in World Championships history, beating Alonso Edward of Panama by over six-tenths of a second. These kinds of

---

10. Christopher Clarey, "Bolt Shatters 100-Meter World Record" (http://www.nytimes.com/2009/08/17/sports/global/17track.html?_r=1).

results don't come out of nowhere. Although there's a certain calm about Bolt's appearance as he runs, in fact he works *hard* to be the best.

After explaining in 1 Corinthians 9:19–23 how he adapts his way of life as much as possible so as to identify with and win to Christ unbelievers from widely varying backgrounds, Paul compares faithful Christian ministry to tenacious athletic training in 9:24–27: "Do you not know that in a race all the runners run, but only one receives the prize? So run that you may obtain it. Every athlete exercises self-control in all things. They do it to receive a perishable wreath, but we an imperishable. So I do not run aimlessly; I do not box as one beating the air. But I discipline my body and keep it under control, lest after preaching to others I myself should be disqualified."

The two key themes here are hard work and the quest for reward. Even though sporting events differ from each other tremendously (e.g., running a race is a profoundly different kind of contest than boxing), they have these two features in common. Only those athletes who are willing to work long and hard can refine their physical and mental skills sufficiently to prevail over their rivals: "No pain, no gain." And such effort is always in pursuit of a prize. Just ask any serious athlete if there's real satisfaction adhering to the motto "It's not whether you win or lose; it's how you play the game." More likely, truly competitive athletes will side with Vince Lombardi: "Winning isn't everything; it's the only thing."

The fact that Paul focuses so much on his own experience in 1 Corinthians 9:19–27 could lead one to think that the strategic effort described is unique to his apostolic calling or, somewhat more generally, to church leadership. But addressing the admonition in 9:24 ("So run that you may obtain it") to all readers suggests otherwise. The charge is to the whole body of Christ; all believers are summoned to a vigorous, all-encompassing pursuit of spiritual exercise as they grow in Christ.

Philippians 3:7–15 speaks of gain and loss in striving to win a prize. Here Paul highlights the focus necessary to succeed in competition. Lesser awards are counted as loss; anything that might keep Paul from "gaining" and "being found in" Christ is considered rubbish. He sounds like a track star straining for the finish line, stretching with every last fiber of his being to cross the tape first and win "the prize of the upward call of God in Christ Jesus." Paul can think of nothing more tragic than to run the race in vain (Galatians 2:2; cf. 5:7; Philippians 2:16).

Let's step back and clarify: What is this prize Paul lunges to grasp? We know it's *not* any kind of self-glory related to his own independent achievement, because the emphasis on the glory and the achievement of Christ won't allow such an interpretation. Paul wants to know Christ (Philippians 3:8—presumably this means to know Christ better than he does already). He longs to gain Christ (again, this can't imply that Christ is absent from his life; the sense, rather, is that there are yet spectacular aspects of being in Christ that Paul yearns to experience). In 3:9 Paul is emphatic that the only righteousness he celebrates is that which he has by faith in Christ. He longs to follow in Jesus' footsteps, both in his suffering and in his resurrection victory. So then, Paul's passionate drive isn't about gaining applause for himself; he's not dreaming of standing on the platform surrounded by cheering fans as a victor's wreath is placed on his head. He's yearning to know Christ and be known by Christ ever more and more. That is his prize.

When he reaches his life's end, Paul looks back over his Christian experience as a great athletic feat: "I have fought the good fight, I have finished the race, I have kept the faith" (2 Timothy 4:7). The contest had been long and hard, as Paul's litany of trials in 2 Corinthians 11:23–28 makes painfully clear. But the effort is "worth it" as he looks ahead to receiving "the crown of righteousness" (2 Timothy 4:8). Is this a vision of spiritual compensation for Paul alone, for church leaders in particular, or for all believers? The rest of the passage answers the question: the crown of righteousness will be awarded not only to Paul, "but also to all who have loved his appearing." All who know and love Christ, long for his final victory, and yearn to be in his eternal presence (i.e., all authentic Christians) will receive this crown as their prize. The reward is the joy of being with Christ.

Hebrews 12:1–2 also provides a picture of the Christian life in athletic imagery: "Therefore, since we are surrounded by so great a cloud of witnesses, let us also lay aside every weight, and sin which clings so closely, and let us run with endurance the race that is set before us, looking to Jesus, the founder and perfecter of our faith, who for the joy that was set before him endured the cross, despising the shame, and is seated at the right hand of the throne of God."

The "cloud of witnesses" in Hebrews 11 (including Abel, Enoch, Noah, Abraham, Moses, Daniel, and others—plus the martyrs who are mentioned) led the way. They gave testimony of God's glory and grace, and the memory of their lives served to bear witness to the Lord. The writer of Hebrews looks back on their inspiring example and then calls on believers to let it arouse them to run the race of faith with all their might, with no distractions or unnecessary burdens to slow them down. And further, let the joy-seeking, cross-enduring model of Jesus motivate a zealous life faith all the way to the finish line.

"To the One Who Conquers"

In Revelation 2–3 the letters to the seven churches of Asia Minor affirm the hard work and endurance of believers there. The Lord commends the church at Ephesus: "I know your works, your toil and your patient endurance, and how you cannot bear with those who are evil, but have tested those who call themselves apostles and are not, and found them to be false. I know you are enduring patiently and bearing up for my name's sake, and you have not grown weary." Identifying and confronting false teachers may be a trying and drawn-out labor of ministry, but it's a vital work deserving of affirmation.

The church at Smyrna endures tribulation, poverty, and slander from those who are opponents of the gospel. What's more, the threat of suffering, imprisonment, and possible death lies ahead. Even so, the Lord urges these believers not to be afraid but to be assured of the promised "crown of life." The church at Thyatira is commended for diligent ministry labors ("I know your works, your love and faith and service and patient endurance, and that your latter works exceed the first"), even though these words are followed by a rebuke for tolerating sin. And the church at Philadelphia is affirmed for its perseverance: "Because you have kept my word about patient endurance, I will keep you from the hour of trial that is coming on the whole world, to try those who dwell on the earth."

From these letters you get the impression that being faithful as the church means facing pressure and enduring trials (even potentially life-threatening tribulations). It takes hard work; there's a battle to fight. Of course, each of the seven letters ends with a promise of blessing to those who prevail in spiritual warfare: "To the one who conquers I will grant to eat of the tree of life, which is in the paradise of God." Spiritual labors may be arduous, but they're not in vain.

Soul Work

These vignettes from Revelation, along with the major biblical themes of warfare, work, and athletic competition summarized above, help us understand the relationship between indwelling sin and the call to holiness: the trek of sanctification is strenuous and the path is steep, so expecting spiritual growth apart from serious "soul work" would be naive. Of course, such effort on our part doesn't merit the Lord's favor; we're saved by grace through faith. But faith works (James 2:14–26), and genuine trust in Christ leads to changed living (see further chapter 2). So the professing believer who doesn't accept the biblical call to a life of devotion and spiritual labor is missing essential aspects of what it means to know God.

Moreover, this labor is *not* a light or casual endeavor, but a most serious undertaking. This is clearly implied by the three analogies before us. Vocational labor is a matter of putting bread on the table. The farmer doesn't treat plowing, planting, cultivating, and harvesting casually—such work is survival. And athletic competition involves striving with all one's might to win. Further, talk of warfare brings sobering connotations of life and death. In light of this, the God-ordained labor of spiritual growth must be embraced as an urgent priority. The work of striving for holiness and mortifying sin is no mere "icing on the cake"—it is the cake.

Further, the war, work, and athletic dimensions of Christian living are ongoing. There may be sudden surges in pursuit of Christ (e.g., at times of special worship or perhaps at major turning points in life), but the labor of spiritual growth is a long-term undertaking; it's a way of life. This, naturally, counts against any "binge" concept of soul work. The pursuit of holiness is more of a marathon than a sprint. There's always a need for further progress in becoming conformed to the image of God's Son (Romans 8:29).

The labor of spiritual growth is also a worthwhile undertaking, to say the least. Losses incurred in warfare may be very great, but the potential gains of protecting family and fellow citizens and of throwing off unjust or tyrannical rulers are of immense value—one might say priceless. Further, working hard puts bread on the table, and that too has profound value. With athletes, though the rigors of training are great, the victor's prize makes all the work worthwhile. And if literal warfare, work, and athletic endeavors yield valuable prizes, how much more so will the vigilant labor of soul formation yield treasured gains for the believer and the church?

Chapter 5

GROWING UP:
ON THE JOURNEY WITH CHRIST

A robin built her nest in an evergreen tree near our house, and to keep a distance from the threatening world below, the nest was situated about twelve feet above the ground. What this cautious bird failed to consider, however, is that our elevated deck brushes up against the other side of the evergreen, so her nest was right at eye level for curious human observers. We saw the four turquoise eggs, and then after a few weeks the sounds of little ones caught our attention. The newly hatched robins were small, wobbly, and very short on feathers. But quickly they learned to look up with open mouths, hopeful of getting a meal. Of course, young birds can't stay in the nest for long—they get too big, and when the mother pushes them out they must learn to fly. Our feathered neighbors soon left their home in the evergreen and ventured out into a big, wide world.

Growth is a sign of health; lack of growth is a signal that something's wrong. Organisms of all kinds go through stages of development. But with growth—biological and spiritual—comes change, and that can be unsettling. We run into growing pains, both literally and figuratively. How do we respond? In fear or anger or by clinging to an earlier life stage? Or will we welcome the new order and look for opportunities it brings? Even though not all physical or spiritual changes are pleasant, as a wise and loving Father, God leads his children through the necessary stages of spiritual formation so they can take flight.

The Bible often speaks of *spiritual* progress in terms of growth. But the comparison to physical development breaks down if it's pushed too far. Physical maturation continues through adolescence and into early adulthood, and then we're "all grown up"—development is over and done. But spiritual maturation, as we shall see, is lifelong; believers are never done growing this side of heaven. What's more, spiritual development can plateau and stagnate or even slide backward, while biological growth relentlessly moves us toward physical maturity.

The Letter to the Hebrews offers a window into a Christian community in which the life of faith had stalled—believers were "stuck" at an early developmental stage, and there they stayed. These Christians were saying no to spiritual progress: "No, thank you; we'll stay right where we are; we like it in this nest."

> About this we have much to say, and it is hard to explain, since you have become dull of hearing. For though by this time you ought to be teachers, you need someone to teach you again the basic principles of the oracles of God. You need milk, not solid food, for everyone who lives on milk is unskilled in the word of righteousness, since he is a child. But solid food is for the mature, for those who have their powers of discernment trained by constant practice to distinguish good from evil.
>
> Therefore let us leave the elementary doctrine of Christ and go on to maturity, not laying again a foundation of repentance from dead works and of faith toward God, and of instruction about washings, the laying on of hands, the resurrection of the dead, and eternal judgment. And this we will do if God permits. (Hebrews 5:11–6:3)

The Spiritual Condition of the Readers

It's important to know a little bit about the Hebrews (i.e., Jewish Christians) who first received this letter. The message is saturated in Old Testament quotations showing how Jesus Christ fulfills all the grand hopes of ancient Israel. Trouble is, persecution had broken out against these Hebrew Christians; they'd endured painful struggles, sufferings, and the plundering of their property (Hebrews 10:32–34), and some of them had even been imprisoned (13:3). In the face of terrifying persecution, these believers were tempted to turn back to what seemed to be a *safe* form of Judaism. After all, ancient Judaism was a legal religion in the Roman Empire, but the new "Jesus movement" was under fire—especially later in the first century when there were major outbreaks of violence against Christians.

The writer, in effect, is pleading, "Don't go back to a Judaism without your Messiah—the loss would be incalculable!" The thrust of the letter, then, is to pile up arguments *not* to turn back: Christ is superior to the angels, to Moses, to Joshua, to the priesthood, and to the old covenant; it's not "worth it" to retreat. But the pressure of persecution brings their spiritual immaturity to the surface. It's easy to be religious when times are good, but take a beating from thugs and have your house burned to the ground, and then you'll see what your faith is really made of.

There's much to tell the Hebrews about "this" (Hebrews 5:11), that is, about how Christ is the ultimate high priest foreshadowed in the ancient Scriptures (5:1–10). The way Jesus brings Old Testament hope to completion is exquisite, but these believers can't appreciate such richness because they're "dull of hearing"—their grasp of God's truth is shallow. As a result, they can't receive the encouragement they most need in the hour of tribulation.

For churches to be healthy, believers must be deeply rooted in God's "word" (vv. 12–13). And that means more than knowing Bible content. Christians need critical thinking skills in order to form consistent beliefs based on Scripture, as well as skills of interpretation to read responsibly and grasp the coherence of God's revelation. And we need agile minds able to assess competing intellectual claims and worldviews such as philosophical naturalism, postmodernism, multi-culturalism, and pluralism—minds prepared to sift out the positive insights as well as flaws inherent in such perspectives. Cognitive skills aren't everything, but believers who lack them and churches that don't cultivate them will remain stunted and vulnerable as spiritual toddlers.

These Hebrew believers have to repeat first grade, as it were, in the school of spiritual growth by being retaught the "the basic principles of the oracles of God" (Hebrews 5:12). It isn't that they're bogged down in Advanced Astrophysics. The class is more basic: Biblical Theology 101, Christ and the Covenants (i.e., the plot of the Bible). In the school of Christ, one can't just skip over certain subjects and still graduate; God's people must grasp the coherence of his story in order to grow and advance.

When you build a house, you simply have to get the foundation right. Footings that aren't level or square, or that rest on soft ground, will lead to disaster later on. A brand-new house built in our neighbor-hood had to be bulldozed, and the builders had to "eat" the enormous expense of starting over because the structure's foundation had settled and then cracked. Never mind that the entire construction project had been completed, carpeting and all, when the flaw started to show. It was a wreck—like a car with a bent chassis that has been "totaled." So too, when it comes to spiritual development, the foundations must be square and solid.

In Hebrews 6:1 the readers are urged to move beyond basic teach-ings so that foundations wouldn't have to be laid yet again. These believers were stuck in the rut of "elementary doctrine" (e.g., repen-tance and faith, resurrection and judgment)—crucial affirmations, to be sure, but basic. It's like they started a marathon, ran the first mile, came to a big hill, sat down to rest, and never got up to run again. The Letter to the Hebrews warns against a spirituality that endlessly rehearses the basics, but fails to "go on to maturity" in learning, wis-dom, and love.

Milk is a remarkable food—God designed a very sophisticated system to feed babies. The nutrients in milk, like protein and calcium, are exactly what newborns need to grow through their first year and beyond. But somewhere in those early years children begin to need solid food. In fact, without solid food, a growing child will be deprived of needed nourishment.

And yet, the believers receiving this letter hadn't yet been weaned off of "milk" (Hebrews 5:12)—they weren't ready for solid spiritual food. To appreciate the significance of failing to "go on to maturity" (6:1) in Christ, consider, by way of comparison, the risks of remaining at an early developmental stage. Would we send a toddler to the neighbors' to borrow a cup of sugar? Do you trust your toddler to cut the grass? Would you put your baby on the subway to make a trip across town? Of course not—it's a recipe for disaster. The necessary skills just aren't there yet—and our children would be in great danger!

Lagging Behind on the Growth Charts

This text raises another question: What level of maturity should these believers have reached? Verse 12 asserts, "By this time you ought to be teachers." *By this time.* There's a divine timetable for spiritual growth, a standard of "normal degree progress." It's *not okay* to take three years to complete eighth grade, and in spiritual life it's *not okay* to delay learning indefinitely and thus never be ready to teach. God has a schedule for spiritual maturation, and believers cause harm to themselves and their churches when they don't graduate "on time."

Healthy spiritual growth involves becoming able to teach the rich, deep truths of the Bible to your children, friends, relatives, neighbors—informally over coffee, in a Bible study, and so on. Of course, not everyone has a special *gift* of teaching, but all mature believers must be able to convey God's truth. A false humility says, "Oh, I could never teach others, I'm just a simple Christian." But every Christian should be able to teach. That doesn't mean "having all the answers." Every teacher is also a student, and Christian instruction is the work of leading fellow students in the exploration of God's truth. The Lord calls his people to be ready to give a defense of their hope in Christ (1 Peter 3:15). Bible-based churches must help all their people grow in knowledge and discernment and become fit to teach. Thus "teacher training" should be central to the discipleship plan of all believers.

So the recipients of Hebrews should have been teachers "by now," and they should have been able to take solid food. "Solid food is for the mature" (5:14)—for those who do their spiritual exercises, training their minds and hearts through "constant practice"—that is, through ongoing study and learning, instilling God's truth for life. Athletes who want to excel practice long and hard. Tennis players stand out in the sun and hit a thousand crosscourt forehands against the ball machine—you practice and practice until you get it right. So too, those who mean business about following Jesus commit themselves to spiritual disciplines like study, meditation, prayer, and fasting (see further chapter 7).

This kind of training allows believers "to distinguish good from evil" (v. 14). The solid food of in-depth learning from God's Word helps growing Christians discern right doctrine from misleading half-truths, distinguish right morals from slippery revisions of God's standards, and anticipate consequences that would come from following a fresh idea. The church needs mature believers with sharp discernment skills who are fully alert to the rich heritage of doctrine and cutting-edge ideas!

In an interview in the *Boston Globe*, author and pastor Rob Bell was asked, "OK, how would you describe what it is that you believe?" He answered, "I embrace the term evangelical, if by that we mean a belief that we together can actually work for change in the world, caring for the environment, extending to the poor generosity and kindness, a hopeful outlook. That's a beautiful sort of thing."[1] Bell had a grand opportunity to spotlight the glory of Christ and the wonder

---

1. Michael Paulson, "Rob Bell on Faith, Suffering, and Christians" (http://www.boston.com/news/local/articles_of_faith/2009/09/rob_bell.html).

of God's saving grace to rescue us from sin's guilt, but he botched it. Kevin DeYoung rightly contends that Bell's description is "devoid of any theological or historical meaning."[2] Today's church needs leaders *and members* with the biblical savvy to see that Bell's talk does little more than recycle tired old ideas that substitute social action for a supernatural Christ. But in many quarters, that kind of discernment is a scarce commodity.

The Challenge to Grow Up

God's Word in Hebrews 5:11–6:3 challenges believers to grow deep in faith and knowledge, strong in wisdom and discernment, and steady in the application of truth as a daily practice. Growing up in Christ means leaving certain things behind: "Let us leave the elementary teachings about Christ" (6:1 NIV)—not in the sense of abandoning them, but by building on them. When you graduate from high school, you don't start from scratch in college but instead build on your foundations. College calculus draws on the lessons of high school algebra. So, believers are summoned to graduate from the basic facts of faith and repentance and the elementary truths of Christ's death and resurrection. This takes place as they explore the glorious world of a rich and deep Bible-based theology.

Believers need to move ahead (6:1): "Let us . . . go on to maturity." What does spiritual maturity involve? Certainly a key aspect is knowledge grounded in understanding the truths of God's Word. To cultivate such knowledge, believers should be involved in Bible study—on their own and with groups. It's wise, as well, to read and wrestle with theology, history, ethics, and hermeneutics, not to mention classic Christian works like Augustine's *Confessions*, Bunyan's *Pilgrim's Progress,* and Edwards's *Religious Affections.* Growing believers will want to read not just easy or familiar Christian works, but also those that are demanding (academically and spiritually). Such

---

2. Kevin DeYoung, "This Is Not Good" (http://thegospelcoalition.org/blogs/kevindeyoung/?s=rob+bell).

a practice of reflecting on biblical truth in light of the rich heritage of Christian literature helps maturing believers advance in wisdom and discernment. Ron Julian clarifies, however, that while maturity involves being deeply committed to the most important truths, it doesn't imply we're free from the temptations of the flesh.[3]

In addition, Hebrews 6:3 makes a crucial point about the need to graduate from elementary things: "And this we will do if God permits." God's will and power are primary in the formation of souls. Spiritual growth happens, ultimately, at the pleasure of God. Paul puts it this way in 1 Corinthians 3:6: "I planted, Apollos watered, but God gave the growth." Only God can bring about authentic spiritual maturation. Ambitious Christians may *say* that they lay claim on maturity or attain spiritual mastery, but in the end it's only God who brings about meaningful growth. And that, of course, amounts to an invitation to pray to the One who is able to do more than all we ask or imagine.

Making Sense of Maturity

In 1 Corinthians 3 Paul confronts a problem similar to that addressed in Hebrews: the Corinthians also were failing to grow spiritually and thus remained on a diet of milk. In their case, the immaturity showed itself in jealousy and strife rather than doctrinal naiveté and retreating from Christ amid trials. A spirit of partisanship ran rampant in the church ("I follow Paul"; "I follow Apollos"). Progress toward maturity would come only when God's people humbly accepted the fact they weren't "anything": "So neither he who plants nor he who waters is anything, but only God who gives the growth" (1 Corinthians 3:7).

---

3. Ron Julian, *Righteous Sinners: The Believer's Struggle with Faith, Grace, and Works* (Colorado Springs: NavPress, 1998), 120. Similarly, Craig Massey contends that spiritual maturity comes as we learn to keep our lives under the direction of the new nature and have fewer and fewer derailments due to the old nature—so it's a matter of progressing in the right direction (*The War within You: A Study of the Believer's Two Natures* (Chicago: Moody, 1987), 58; cf. J. C. Ryle, *Holiness* in J. I. Packer, *Faithfulness and Holiness: The Witness of J. C. Ryle* (Wheaton: Crossway, 2002), 190).

And yet, it's not as if Paul thinks some decisive act will finally "do it." A stride of maturation in one area would, no doubt, allow other growth needs to be seen. Paul himself, decades into his own spiritual formation, writes to the Philippians, "Not that I have already obtained this [i.e., a deeper knowledge of Christ] or am already perfect, but I press on to make it my own, because Christ Jesus has made me his own" (3:12). Just one literary breath later, however, the imperfect apostle doesn't hesitate to make his own spiritual life an example for the Philippian Christians who are "mature" to follow. Spiritual maturation isn't about achieving flawlessness, but about growing in faith and holiness and abounding in love more and more.[4] Sanctification involves the ongoing process by which "we all, with unveiled face, beholding the glory of the Lord, are being transformed into the same image from one degree of glory to another" (2 Corinthians 3:18).

In Ephesians Paul addresses the relationship between church leadership and spiritual growth in the body. Maturing pastors, teachers, and other church leaders resist the temptation to keep a tight grip on all aspects of church activity, but instead they "equip the saints for the work of ministry" (4:12). They minister not just *to* people but *through* people. And they do so with this goal: "until we all attain to the unity of the faith and of the knowledge of the Son of God, to mature manhood, to the measure of the stature of the fullness of Christ, so that we may no longer be children, tossed to and fro by the waves and carried about by every wind of doctrine, by human cunning, by craftiness in deceitful schemes" (4:13–14). Correspondingly, Christians who are

---

4. J. C. Ryle maintains that one can measure growth in grace by (1) increased humility; (2) increased faith and love toward Christ; (3) increased holiness of life and conversation; (4) increased spirituality of taste and mind; (5) increase of charity; and (6) increased zeal in trying to do good to souls (in Packer, *Faithfulness and Holiness*, 192–94). Bruce Demarest clarifies that the *teleioi* (i.e., the "mature," Phil. 3:15) aren't perfect but have made appropriate progress in spiritual growth (*The Cross and Salvation*, 419). M. Craig Barnes states that progress on journey home is measured by how far your face has turned from down to up (*Searching for Home: Spirituality for Restless Souls* [Grand Rapids: Brazos, 2003], 105).

not maturing are vulnerable to being deceived and prone to get truth and love out of balance. Churches need pastors and teachers who expound biblical truth and identify threats of error and who equip and mobilize their people to take such ministries forward.

In his second letter, the apostle Peter, sensing that his own death is soon to come (2 Peter 1:14–15), puts an emphasis on the urgency of spiritual growth for his readers. For example, if their godliness, faith, and knowledge "are increasing, they keep you from being ineffective or unfruitful in the knowledge of our Lord Jesus Christ" (1:7–8). Growing in Christlikeness, progressing in faith and holiness—this is what spiritual maturity "looks like." By contrast, it's not said that believers must have attained absolute godliness in order to be effective and fruitful in ministry. The letter concludes with the exhortation to "grow in the grace and knowledge of our Lord and Savior Jesus Christ." Such spiritual progress will keep the church from being swept up in error, thus bringing glory to the Lord.

In the New Testament picture, then, spiritual maturity involves progress in faith and the knowledge of Jesus Christ. The "mature" believer is, in actuality, one who is matur*ing*. As we've already seen, the Bible doesn't encourage believers to expect to reach perfection in this life (chapter 3). We *aim* at holiness and *aspire* to walk in the steps of Jesus, and, by God's help, in this way we grow in Christ.[5] In fact, it's implied, as John Calvin correctly asserts: "So long as there is daily progress there cannot be perfection."[6] In other words, even if one is advancing in spiritual growth by leaps and bounds, the fact that there will still be room for improvement tomorrow means that perfection is not yet reached.

---

5. Cf. G. B. Caird and L. D. Hurst, *New Testament Theology* (Oxford: Clarendon Press, 1994), 122–25. Perfectionism, in fact, is an expression of spiritual immaturity (Donald McCullough, *The Consolations of Imperfection*, 69).

6. Quoted in R. S. Wallace, *Calvin's Doctrine of the Christian Life* (Edinburgh: Oliver and Boyd, 1959), 323.

At the same time, an absence of growth should be alarming. As J. C. Ryle observes, "The Christian who is always at a standstill, to all appearances the same man, with the same little faults, and weaknesses, and besetting sins, and petty infirmities, is seldom the Christian who does much good. The man who shakes and stirs minds, and sets the world thinking, is the believer who is continually improving and going forward."[7] By contrast, Ryle adds, "One of the surest marks of spiritual decline is a decreased interest about the souls of others and the growth of Christ's kingdom."[8] When complacency seeps into the believer's heart or despair clouds over the soul, the need of the hour is to draw near to God (James 4:8), seeking a fresh work of the Spirit to bring hope and progress in holiness.

The Journey of Spiritual Formation

Along with images of growth, the developmental spirituality of the New Testament is depicted by various travel motifs. When Jesus summons bystanders to "follow me" (e.g., Mark 1:16–20), he calls them to a literal trek then and there in the Palestinian countryside. But "following Jesus" is also a metaphor for devotion and discipleship. For example, in Luke 9:23, Jesus announces, "If anyone would come after me, let him deny himself and take up his cross daily and follow me." In this case, following involves a certain kind of spiritual response to Jesus encompassing self-denial and daily cross bearing. Following Jesus is a way of life, a spiritual journey, in which sin is continuously and progressively, even if imperfectly, put to death.

The extended travel narrative highlighted in Luke's gospel, in which Jesus is en route to Jerusalem (9:51–19:27), portrays the bulk of his public ministry as a journey toward Jerusalem and the cross, and then on to his heavenly Father in glory. In Luke's sequel, the Acts

---

7. J. C. Ryle, *Holiness* [in Packer, *Faithfulness and Holiness*], 191.
8. Ibid., 194.

of the Apostles, the travel motif turns outward from Jerusalem toward "the end of the earth" (1:8). Progressively the narrative moves through Judea and Samaria, and then into Asia Minor, Macedonia, Achaia, stretching on finally to Rome. In this way the church is pictured as a fellowship on the move, a transformed people with a mission and a map.

Of course, this literal trek parallels the journey of faith and discipleship for believers who are called to trust in the Lord even as persecution propels them outward from Jerusalem (Acts 8:1, 4). The church is even identified as "the Way" (e.g., 9:2; 19:9, 23; 24:14, 22—the Greek term is sometimes translated "road" or "path"). To be God's people means to live not as settlers but sojourners, venturing through this world. The life of faith, at root, is a journey of spiritual development; it's not so much that we arrive as that we're "on the way."[9]

Along this long and winding discipleship road, Christians typically pass through stages of spiritual maturation, some of which can be very trying. St. John of the Cross speaks of the soul's "dark night," a seeming impasse of spiritual barrenness in which God, though once vividly present, now seems to be distant and remote. Faith in Christ during the joyous seasons early in the spiritual pilgrimage is very different from the humbled, broken dependence on the Lord that survives the dark night.[10]

Adoniram and Nancy Judson, sharing a deep faith in Christ and a compelling call to bring the gospel to the lost, sailed from the United

---

9. Mortification of sin is a lifelong process, and it does not bring the final elimination of sin in this life (Owen, *Sin and Temptation*, 154; cf. Phil. 3:12). Victory comes by degrees and over time; it is only realized progressively (Richard Sibbes, *The Bruised Reed* [Puritan Paperbacks; Edinburgh: Banner of Truth, 1998], 93–95, 99, 101, 106).

10. See, e.g., Robert Guelich and Janet Hagberg, *The Critical Journey: Stages in the Life of Faith* (Salem, WI: Sheffield, 1995), 113–30 (they tell of the shattering experience of hitting "the wall"). Surprisingly, Dallas Willard (*The Divine Conspiracy: Rediscovering Our Hidden Life in God* [San Francisco: Harper, 1998], 367–69) does not speak of a dark night when describing the stages of spiritual progress.

States to Burma in 1812. But they encountered dreadful suffering, including death in infancy for all three of their children. Adoniram was arrested in 1824 in the wake of an anti-British movement in Burma, imprisoned to face atrocious conditions, and later driven on a death march across the land. Finally, after a year and a half in captivity, he was released and put to work translating negotiations between Burma and Britain. Only a few months later Nancy died of fever.

Overwhelmed by grief, Judson threw himself into mission work. But his heart wasn't in it, and he slid into a deep depression, abandoning his mission colleagues to live in a hut in the jungle. "Spiritual desolation engulfed him: 'God is to me the Great Unknown. I believe in him, but I find him not.'"[11] His dark night went on for three years. By God's grace and through a great outpouring of love and prayer from mission coworkers and Burmese believers, Judson recovered and actually acquired a new depth of faith that intensified his ministry.

In the dark night it's as if the Lord steps away. The believer feels isolated and abandoned, finding prayer most difficult in this arid place.[12] "What has happened is that everything is lost and gone. All that is left is the stripped human will, unsupported, unadorned, without reinforcement or reward."[13] But in this process, in fact, God is assisting his people in letting go of any experience or satisfaction they trust more than him.[14] Believers facing a "dark night" feel confounded; they realize how little they truly love God, yet they also perceive in a new way that the world and its pleasures cannot satisfy them. All in all, it's an experience of being made to feel helpless, which is just where God wants his maturing children to be.[15]

---

11. Ruth Tucker, *From Jerusalem to Irian Jaya* (Grand Rapids: Zondervan, 1983), 129.
12. Benedict Groeschel, *Spiritual Passages: The Psychology of Spiritual Development* (New York: Crossroad, 1983), 84.
13. Ibid., 85.
14. John Coe, "Musings on the Dark Night of the Soul: Insights from St. John of the Cross on a Developmental Spirituality," *Journal of Psychology and Theology* 28 (2000): 300.
15. Ibid., 302; cf. 304–306.

To go through the dark night (a "night" that can last years) is potentially dangerous for the believer. The pressure to retreat from growth and fall back into familiar territory is very great. This is a time when close involvement with other disciples is essential and when sound teaching and able spiritual mentoring are most helpful for keeping one's equilibrium. Guelich and Hagberg observe that some who hit "the wall" (i.e., the shattering and humbling experience of coming to the end of the rope spiritually) decide to revert back to an earlier stage of spiritual development and thus never mature beyond that point.[16] And so, they don't break through into a new spiritual realm where God's sustaining presence is vividly known and in which they keenly feel both their own vulnerability and God's sufficiency.

The necessary posture for maturing believers is to be ready for major changes in how the Lord relates to them, prepared to rely on God tenaciously despite shifting life circumstances, staying in his Word and in one another's company, all the while moving through uncharted territory where faith is humbled or even shattered. John Bunyan's elaborate allegory, *Pilgrim's Progress*, depicts sharply differing stages of the journey of faith (e.g., bright pastures and dreary swamps, joyous sunshine and ominous clouds, lovely meadows and sheer cliffs). In light of these widely varying life circumstances, believers need to be flexible about their expectations of how God leads and guides, and helps them mature, during the long spiritual voyage home.

Coming to Terms with Time

Time is the earthly playing field on which the church competes for spiritual growth. The passing of time brings to light dim and hidden corners of our souls that need to be cleaned out and given over to the lordship of Christ. In his well-received booklet *My Heart—Christ's Home*, Robert Boyd Munger envisions the life of spiritual formation

---

16. Guelich and Hagberg, *Critical Journey*, 115; cf. 122.

as the process by which Jesus Christ progressively takes over in every room of the house—the house of one's heart. As the host proceeds to yield one room after another, time reveals a stench—some foul odor hidden in the soul. It's a closet, a small and out-of-the-way room, but it's filled with vile things. Munger wants the reader to feel the tension when all the major rooms of the house have come under the oversight of Christ, but one obscure closet remains a holdout for sin and Satan. Discipleship involves the process of giving over all rooms of one's heart to Christ. But time is necessary, in Munger's allegory, to discover the odious closet. The Lord uses time to test the faith of his people, thus bringing either genuine maturation or lingering weakness to the surface.

God has designed our passage through this world more like a marathon than a sprint so that he can put his finger—for his honor and our good—on the places where sin has a hold. Solomon, the wise and famous king of ancient Israel, becomes a helpful example in this regard. His is a story of spiritual degeneration over time. You might say that time either revealed or yielded a shallowness of devotion to the Lord. Even though he reigned well for an era and excelled in riches and wisdom (1 Kings 10:23), with time his expanding harem brought downfall in spiritual adultery and the worship of other gods. "For when Solomon was old his wives turned away his heart after other gods, and his heart was not wholly true to the LORD his God, as was the heart of David his father" (1 Kings 11:4). This is more than saying, "Nobody's perfect," because the well-known imperfections of David don't keep him from being classified as one who is "wholly true to the LORD his God." Something more devious and culpable is afoot with Solomon. Notice that it's over time (he's become "old") that his "heart" turned away from the Lord.

Midlife is a rite of passage in which a certain disillusionment threatens and aging adults are forced to face up to their not-so-limitless potential. Men buy sailboats and sports cars in midlife to reassure themselves they're still young and dynamic. But one can't hold back the tide of aging forever, and with the advancing of years in Christ, believers may find that their simpler, more confident faith stance from youth is eroding. Time feels like a great enemy, since, of course, we were made for eternity (Ecclesiastes 3:11) in God's presence. But in the drawn-out scheme of spiritual growth during this earthly exile, God uses the passing of days and years to bring our soul sicknesses to the surface so we can confess, repent, and draw yet nearer to him.

As beings made in the image of God, humans are ill at ease under the dominion of time. Something inside us yearns to break free from the bonds of a time-bound life. Sustaining a vibrant, deep, earnest faith in Christ through the seasons is trying. It's as though there were a spiritual version of the second law of thermodynamics that says (to oversimplify a bit) the human heart wears down eventually as the pull of sin intensifies.[17] We feel that our waiting for relief and spiritual consolation has gone on long enough. And yet, the more we insist on earthly comforts to brush aside the harsh effects of passing years, the more difficult it becomes to trust in the goodness of God.[18] The Lord forces us to face pressures of time's passing in order to help us see the pervasive spiritual weakness of our souls, thus driving us to our knees before him in humble, repentant faith. So time is harsh but valuable; waiting is unpleasant but often vital for the maturation process. In this drawn-out ordeal, followers of Christ come to see the truth of their weakness and the splendor of God's grace with new clarity. And that is progress.

---

17. Sin is patient; it lies in wait only to strike at an "opportune" moment. If temptation dies down for a time, do not suppose that the Enemy has given up (John Owen, *Sin and Temptation*, 155–56).

18. Larry Crabb, *Inside Out*, 138.

Chapter 6

PARADOXES OF SPIRITUAL FORMATION

In the movie *The Terminal*, Viktor Navorski is a traveler whose home country of "Krakozhia" is taken over in a military coup while he's en route to New York. As a result, the status of his citizenship is in limbo. It's not safe to go home, but U.S. immigration authorities won't allow this foreigner to enter the country since they don't recognize the new government of Krakozhia. So Navorski's visa and passport are canceled, and he's required to remain in the terminal; JFK International Airport itself becomes his new "home." While patiently living out of a suitcase at Gate 67, Navorski finds creative ways to cope—and he learns a good bit of English while being detained for weeks and even months. The story is striking because so many people are familiar with the airport environment, and yet no one thinks of it as a final destination. Airports are just places we pass through.

And yet, odd as Navorski's situation seems, it can be a parable of the Christian life: We're required to have an extended "layover" here and now while on the way to heaven. We're travelers, and the present life is our journey. On this venture, believers have certain practices that belong to the future world and others rooted in this present age. And that creates tension.

God's reign is "now but not yet," and our calling is to live "in but not of the world." With our in-transit lifestyle, we need to hold two impulses in balance: yearning, striving, and passionately pursuing the glories of the life to come (making us restless), yet also learning to walk in God's peace, forsake anxiety, and be content (making us restful). There's a tension between these two necessary facets of the Christian experience. Stillness and striving hold hands in paradoxical partnership in the journey of spiritual formation.

Restless: Pressing On

In Philippians 3–4, Paul commends to his readers a careful combination of restlessness and restfulness. Believers are to press on *and* be at peace. Is this just double talk? Does the letter send a mixed message about what to expect in the Christian walk? How does it work, in practice, to strain forward vigorously and yet remain content in all circumstances? Can believers be content knowing that impulses of sin have not yet been fully rooted out of their hearts? Can Christians be content as sinners and yet discontent with sinful practices?

Paul's impressive Jewish "resumé" was faultless (Philippians 3:6). He'd excelled in learning God's law, obeying it meticulously, and zealously striving to crush any threat to Judaism. Before encountering the risen Jesus on the road to Damascus (Acts 9:1–9), he'd tried to annihilate the church. But through a blinding clash with omnipotence, everything changed: Paul realized Jesus was indeed Messiah—the divine stamp of approval was unmistakable. Knowing Christ then became the axis of Paul's life; everything revolved around trusting Jesus as Messiah. And so, suddenly his impeccable Jewish heritage seemed relatively unimportant—even "rubbish"—compared to gaining Christ.

In Philippians 3:8–10 Paul talks about his *present* longing. A knowledge of Christ isn't just something acquired at conversion. It's his present and ongoing passion to "gain Christ," "be found" in Christ, and "know" Christ—to know him in his risen power even while bearing the cross and following in his footsteps of suffering. Paul's spiritual zeal is ferocious.

Such fervor, however, is often lacking in the visible church. A. W. Tozer laments the spiritual immaturity of believers who don't pursue God. Being born again is not an end but a beginning, "for now begins the glorious pursuit, the heart's happy exploration of the infinite riches of the Godhead. . . . To have found God and still to pursue Him is the soul's paradox of love."[1] Hanging everything in the Christian life on the initial act of accepting Christ and then craving no further revelation of God to our souls is based on a false logic "which insists that if we have found Him we need no more seek Him."[2] But Paul's vision of Christian experience includes restless, relentless striving.

And yet, as he seeks to know Christ more and more, Paul becomes vividly aware of his own sin. In Philippians 3:12 he concedes, "Not that I have already obtained all this" (there's so much more of the splendor of Christ to explore) and not that I "have already been made perfect" (NIV). What the greatest theologian and pioneer missionary in the history of the church is saying here is that *he has not "arrived."* Paul the apostle, late in his life and decades after coming to faith in Christ, is still a work in progress, still growing.

I'm a Wimbledon fanatic, so there are a lot of great tennis battles stored away on my mental hard drive—like the epic clash of Roger Federer and Rafael Nadal in 2008, which many consider the greatest tennis match of all time. I also remember Andre Agassi versus Goran Ivanisevic in 1992, another fierce five-set battle: quick, tireless Aggasi returning serve and firing ground strokes from the base line, and

---

1. A. W. Tozer, *Pursuit of God*, 14–15.
2. Ibid., 16.

explosive, cannon-serve Ivanisevic blasting away. Agassi persevered in a marathon match and took his place atop the tennis world that year.

But you don't get to the top without a lot of hard work. For Agassi it began in early childhood. As a grade-school boy he would hit three thousand to five thousand tennis balls *a day*, striving and straining to get better and better, to be the best, pressing on. In a parallel way, faith in Christ presses on in sanctified ambition "toward the goal to win the prize for which God has called me heavenward in Christ Jesus" (Philippians 3:14 NIV). Restlessness is vital for spiritual growth; the Lord hasn't put us here to casually coast, but to strain forward toward the finish line.

Restful: At Peace

However, authentic Christian spirituality also encompasses a call to contentment: "Do not be anxious about anything, but in everything by prayer and supplication with thanksgiving let your requests be made known to God" (Philippians 4:6). In other words, replace worry with prayer. In 1989 Bobby McFerrin won a Grammy for his hit song "Don't Worry, Be Happy." But there's so much more to Philippians 4:6 than a "pick me up" pep talk. The key distinction is the reason to pray and not worry: *because* a wise, loving, strong heavenly Father beckons his people to pray and *because* he calls his children into a lifestyle of joy (v. 4) and thankfulness (v. 6).

Philippians 4:7 goes on: "And the peace of God, which surpasses all understanding, will guard your hearts and your minds in Christ Jesus." Believers can know the peace of God because they rely on the God of peace. Christian peace isn't a mere cease-fire or a general sense of serenity. It's God's peace, a tranquility of heart because God is above, before, below, beneath, beside his people at all times. What's more, Christian peace "surpasses all understanding." This is not to suggest that it's irrational, but instead that it's more than rational, more than just a truth to affirm. God's peace pervades one's whole being, generating deep rest.

"Contentment" is how Paul puts it in Philippians 4:11: "Not that I am speaking of being in need, for I have learned in whatever situation I am to be content." He thanks the Philippians for contributing to his financial support in verse 10, but then in verse 17 he clarifies that he hasn't been sitting around, moaning by the mailbox, waiting for their check to come so he could finally breathe easily and relax. Not at all. He's at rest no matter what, check or no check.

Paul elaborates, "Not that I am speaking of being in need . . ." Wait a minute—he's *not* in need? Philippians is one of the Prison Letters—Paul writes with chains on and thinks he may soon be executed (1:17, 20). Most of us would say he *is* in need. But Paul's not unraveled even by the threat of death. To live is Christ and to die is gain (1:21)—he can't lose. Here's the testimony of a believer who trusts Christ and disregards his earthly circumstances. Even if he's executed, Paul realizes that God will use such things for good.

When I ran into job loss a few years ago and the income stream dried up, our family struggled to be content. After leaving a ministry position and seeking God's leading to a new opportunity, I was coming up empty-handed. Suitable openings just weren't panning out. As time passed, I did odd jobs to pay the bills and help keep the family afloat, and Cheryl also took a part-time job to help put bread on the table. Neither of us was doing a type of work that remotely matched our training and interests. On many occasions we'd pray and let the Lord know this dry spell had gone on "long enough" (good of us to tell God this, wasn't it?). But his timetable was simply much different from ours.

Paul tells of being content "in any and every circumstance" (Philippians 4:12). That didn't come to us naturally—the natural (and sinful) impulse of my heart is to fear and blame and imagine all sorts of worst-case scenarios. I can anticipate all kinds of things that could go wrong. And yet, despite my inconsistent faith, the Lord helped our family move toward contentment. He met our needs, often in surprising ways, reminding us of his presence and sovereign oversight in our desert experience. In fact, with hindsight we've come to see ways that our adversities were good for our hearts and helpful in preparation for subsequent ministry.

Philippians 4 raises many questions for the believer: Have I learned the secret of being content in all situations? Am I content whether well fed or hungry? Am I content with plenty—thanking God for those seasons of "more than enough" without demanding that my lifestyle keep going up and up—and content with want, with lack, even with poverty? The underlying issue here relating to the believer's level of spiritual maturation is *trust*: When wealth comes, do we transfer our trust to it? And when hard times hit, do we give up on God and assume he doesn't care or has lost control? Both prosperity and poverty threaten the believer's faith in God's wise and loving oversight.[3]

Passage and Portion

We need to put Philippians 3 and 4 together. Paul was a brilliant theologian writing under the inspiration of the Holy Spirit, and yet he's given us two chapters that stand in a certain tension. With careful reflection, however, we can see how they dovetail together:

- In terms of closeness to Christ, we always need to grow. The more we advance in faith and understanding, the more we see the true wonders of the Lord. And that inspires further yearning to know and savor Christ. So we seek and strive for the joy of reveling in the presence of the Lord (Philippians 3). Maturing believers are restless; they press on.

- But in terms of outward circumstances in life, we can accept "whatever" (Philippians 4). Christ-followers need to see that investment portfolios or home alarms or insurance policies don't provide any lasting security.

---

3. On trust and anxiety, see also Matt. 6:25–34; 11:28–30; 1 Peter 5:7.

If we have Christ, wealth is no gain in comparison, and neither is health or safety. And if we have Christ, poverty or affliction is no loss in comparison. Maturing believers are restful; they have peace.

In 1648 Jeremiah Burroughs pointed to this paradox or "mystery" of contentment: "Mark, here lies the mystery of it, a little in the world will content a Christian for his *passage*, but all the world, and ten thousand times more, will not content a Christian for his *portion*."[4] He distinguishes "passage" from "portion." For the Christian's brief *passage* through this life on the journey to heaven, God says to be content even with bare bones (Philippians 4). But when it comes to the believer's ultimate *portion* (i.e., eternal destiny), one mustn't settle for anything less than the very presence and fullness of God (Philippians 3), content with little of earthly rewards, but never content without the everlasting love of Christ.

When God's people keep zeal and rest in balance, they can make great strides of spiritual growth. And what's more, two dangerous errors are avoided: First, contentment doesn't degenerate into passivity. God doesn't call believers to a lazy spirituality. Nor should they be careless about other people's pain; loving neighbors means striving to help, serve, and relieve their suffering through the love of Christ. Second, striving won't get twisted into legalism that works to earn God's favor. We "press on" to know Christ better and to grow in faith and obedience *because* we're already forgiven, not to gain points with God—his love is a gift!

A vital clarification for sorting out the message of Philippians 3–4 is that although believers are summoned to a life of contentment even now—even here in this life in which we're still sinners—God's Word doesn't invite us to be content with sin itself. This would be twisting

---

4. Jeremiah Burroughs, *The Rare Jewel of Christian Contentment* (Puritan Paperbacks; Edinburgh: Banner of Truth, 1964), 43, italics original.

contentment (which is grounded in trust) into complacency (which turns away from the Lord). And it would be pitting one Pauline text against others that speak of imitating God and battling against sin and Satan (e.g., Ephesians 5:1; 6:10–20). The call to contentment has to do with earthly circumstances, such as Paul's chains, and not with one's lingering sin.

Nevertheless, a proper Christian contentment must come to terms with God's design in the outworking of his salvation plan that involves our gradual growth in holiness and progressive sanctification rather than instantaneous and absolute holiness at the moment of justification. In other words, there's a rightful sense of being content to live as a sinner while battling fiercely against acts of sin. This is a fine distinction, and misconstruing it can lead to calamity. So let me restate: The biblical summons of Christian disciples to a lifestyle of contentment in Christ does not mean declaring a truce with sin (the battle is lifelong) or making excuses about one's besetting sins, saying, "That's just the way I am." But it does mean being at peace with our sovereign God's scheme of salvation history in which we journey with Jesus, even though our souls have so far to go to be brought into conformity with his glorious image (see further chapter 11).

When It Doesn't Feel Like Progress

If we return to the idea of spiritual formation as a journey, yet another paradox surfaces when people assume the path of progress should be relatively "straight" with a gentle but steady incline. But, in fact, maturation commonly follows a twisting road with sharp turns and unanticipated switchbacks along the way. If there were a graph to track growth in holiness, it would show various dips and spikes over time. Of course, that line should have at least a generally upward trajectory, suggesting some greater insight and godliness for believers with the passing of life's seasons. But even this expectation may be too simplistic.[5] For example, a gain in godliness may appear to others very different from the way it looks to the believer going through the fires of refinement. Perspective makes a major difference in assessing the presence or degree of spiritual maturation.

In an article on spirituality, I offered this illustration: "Imagine the novice mountain climber setting out to scale the grand peak called Holiness. Although the summit isn't visible from base camp, the eager mountaineer imagines that it can't be 'that far' away. It's only after ascending well beyond the foothills that the majestic summit finally comes into view, and it leaves the climber's jaw hanging. A true sense of the scale of the venture begins to register."[6]

Numerous Christians through the ages have encountered this kind of paradox on the spiritual formation journey, saying (in one way or another) that the more you mature in Christ, the more you become aware of your lingering immaturity and indwelling sin. In other words, an effect of meaningful progress in holiness is becoming aware, possibly brutally aware, of sin's pervasive presence in one's own heart and lifestyle—hideous impulses and attitudes that previously had gone unnoticed. This observation has been articulated in a variety of ways:

- John Calvin: "The more eminently anyone excels in holiness, the farther he feels from perfect righteousness, and the more clearly he perceives that he can trust in nothing but the mercy of God alone" (quoted by R. S. Wallace, *Calvin's Doctrine of the Christian Life*, 323).

- Richard Sibbes: "Thirdly, the more grace, the more spiritual life, and the more spiritual life, the more

---

5. David Peterson (*Possessed by God: A New Testament Theology of Sanctification and Holiness* [New Studies in Biblical Theology; Grand Rapids: Eerdmans, 1995], 70) challenges the stair-step image of sanctification, arguing that it can create unrealistic expectations and lead to guilt and despair for believers who don't perceive such progress in their lives.

6. Peter Nelson, "Impractical Christianity," *Christianity Today* (Sept. 2005): 82.

antipathy to the contrary. Therefore, none are so aware of corruption as those whose souls are most alive" (*The Bruised Reed*, 49).

- Joseph Alleine: It's a sign of maturation "if you grow more vile in your own eyes" ("Motives and Marks of Growth in Grace").

- François Fénelon: "Little faults become great, and even monstrous in our eyes, in proportion as the pure light of God increases in us; just as the sun in rising, reveals the true dimensions of objects which were dimly and confusedly discovered during the night" (*Spiritual Progress*, XVI).

- Jonathan Edwards: "In times of the brightest light and highest flight of love and joy, there was found no disposition to the opinion of being now perfectly free from sin . . . but exceedingly the contrary. At such times especially, it was seen how loathsome and polluted the soul is; soul and body, and every act and word, appearing like rottenness and corruption in that pure and holy light of God's glory" ("Thoughts on the Revival," 1.378).

- J. C. Ryle: The most eminent saints "have always had the deepest sense of their own utter unworthiness and imperfection. The more spiritual light they have enjoyed, the more they have seen their own countless defects and shortcomings" (*Holiness* in J. I. Packer, *Faithfulness and Holiness*, 97).[7]

- F. B. Meyer: "The nearer we live to God, the more sensitive we become to the presence of sin. Increasing light means increasing self-judgment; and things which were allowed

---

7. Ryle drives this concept home: "How true it is that the holiest saint is in himself a 'miserable sinner,' and a debtor to mercy and grace to the last moment of his existence!" (J. C. Ryle, *Holiness*, in J. I. Packer, *Faithfulness and Holiness: The Witness of J. C. Ryle* [Wheaton: Crossway, 2002], 112; cf. 123–24, 136, 142, 144, 192, 200).

in the twilight of the dawn, become abhorrent as the noontide light reveals their true character" (*Christian Living*, 58).

- C. S. Lewis: The holier a man is, the more he is aware of his sinfulness (*Problem of Pain*, 67). And about our "muddy and tattered" condition when we reach "home" after ongoing falls into temptation: "It is when we notice the dirt that God is most present in us; it is the very sign of his presence" (in W. H. Lewis, *Letters of C. S. Lewis*, 199).

- John Murray: "Indeed, the more sanctified the person is, the more conformed he is to the image of his Saviour, the more he must recoil against every lack of conformity to the holiness of God. The deeper his apprehension of the majesty of God, the greater the intensity of his love to God, the more persistent his yearning for the attainment of the prize of the high calling of God in Christ Jesus, the more conscious will he be of the gravity of the sin which remains and the more poignant will be his detestation of it" (*Redemption Accomplished and Applied*, 145).

- Richard Lovelace: "New departments of the flesh open up in our lives as we mature" (*Dynamics of Spiritual Life*, 110).

- Jerry Bridges: "A part of growing in holiness is the Holy Spirit's making us aware of the need of holiness" (*The Pursuit of Holiness*, 43). "As we grow in the knowledge of God's holiness, even though we are also growing in the practice of holiness it seems the gap between our knowledge and our holiness always gets wider" (104, italics original).[8]

---

8. See also the interview of Jerry Bridges in *Discipleship Journal* 159 (May–June 2007): 20.

- Wayne Grudem: As Christians grow in maturity, they become aware especially of inward sins of attitude and motive (e.g., pride, selfishness, lack of faith, lack of zeal for God, and failure to trust God in all things) (*Systematic Theology*, 752).
- Larry Crabb: "Those who walk closest to God feel their disappointment most keenly" (*Inside Out*, 86).
- Ron Julian: "In a way, the fact that sometimes we feel like we're getting worse instead of better is more evidence of the change God has brought about. . . . Instead of the glib promises of our youth that we are 'totally sold out to God,' in our maturity we grow much more distrustful of ourselves" (*Righteous Sinners*, 101–2).
- Michael McKinley: "One of the surprises of the Christian life is that as you grow more holy in life and practice, you also grow in your awareness of your own sin and depravity. In fact, the latter is a key to the former. As a result, while you are in reality becoming more sanctified, your daily experience is often that of feeling less sanctified" ("Something for Holy People to Glory In").
- Tim Chester: "We see the dirt in our hearts all the more as we move toward the light of God" (*You Can Change*, 175).

These believers recognize that "progress" in sanctification is not simple or straightforward. Expectations of neat and tidy stair-step advancement have to be challenged. When following Jesus, the way up is down, loss is gain, and death is the doorway to life; in Jesus' upside-down plan of spiritual formation the last shall be first.

This is not to minimize the real possibility of a greater conformity to the image of Christ (Romans 8:29) over time, nor am I offering any basis for excuses, such as, "Sin is inevitable, nothing I can do about it," or "I'm doomed to fall into more and more sin, even though I want to steer clear of it." As the true child of God battles against sin and seeks the Lord's help to grow stronger in faith and obedience, there must *and will be* signs of life transformation. When real faith exists in human hearts, it leads to changed living (see chapter 2; cf. James 2:14–26). The absence of change and the absence of growth and battling and laboring and running to win the prize (etc.) are signs of the absence of Christ in a person's life.

Nevertheless, it remains true that when believers draw nearer to Christ, in the light of his glorious presence their sin becomes increasingly visible and detestable to them. A traditional graph that plots sanctification over time doesn't bring this out. Even if the generally upward trajectory of the line is marked with occasional dips and setbacks, this way of charting spiritual growth cannot reveal the soul dynamic that makes progress feel like its opposite.

Jerry Bridges offers an alternative portrayal:[9]

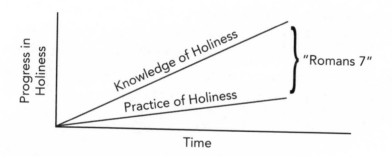

This depiction suggests that while believers may advance in the practice of holiness, their knowledge of the perfect holiness to which they're called (1 Peter 1:15–16) increases at a faster rate, so there's an ever-widening gap between the two.[10] The life of discipleship thus involves

9. Used by permission of the Navigators, taken from Jerry Bridges, *The Pursuit of Holiness*, 2006, all rights reserved, www.navpress.com.
10. The fact that Bridges names this gap "Romans 7" is neither here nor there (cf. chap.

an ongoing and even increasing dissonance between the glorious ideal to which one aspires and the modest reality of how one actually lives.

Many Christians who recognize this gulf, this ever-widening chasm, struggle to come to terms with it and think there must be some way to relieve the tension—to make it "go away." But the tension is perennial in the present life; it's part of normal Christian experience. An effect of getting nose to nose with the paradox that growth often feels like setback is that the believer's heart is humbled. And further, Christ is exalted as the one who, through his active obedience and sacrificial death, deserves *all* credit for our initial justification, progress in discipleship, and final salvation.

Jim Wilhoit takes yet another approach to graphing spiritual progress (or the lack thereof) over time, and the key feature he brings out is the perceived "size" of the cross. Believers need to let the cross of Christ "grow."[11] Our basic difficulty results from two major impairments to spiritual vision that greatly limit perception of our own spiritual brokenness: an inclination toward self-justification and spiritual blindness. Between these two imposing obstructions of the soul's vision, there isn't much space left through which to see the magnitude of our sin problem and ongoing need for grace or to perceive the enormity of God's saving and sanctifying love displayed in the cross of Christ:[12]

---

3 on the interpretation of Rom. 7:14–25); it could just as well have been called "The Christian Struggle" since the reality he describes is supported by an array of biblical texts.

11. James C. Wilhoit, *Spiritual Formation as if the Church Mattered*, 104–13.

12. Ibid., 107.

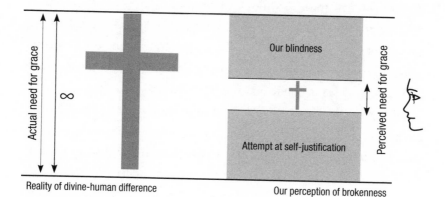

Reality of divine-human difference   Our perception of brokenness

In a series of case studies, Wilhoit then brings out some of the striking differences in how believers respond to the need to "see" the cross clearly. The ideal (i.e., mature) response involves growing more humble, seeing one's own sin with sharp clarity, recognizing God's breathtaking holiness, and, in this way, by God's help, "letting" the cross loom large and virtually fill one's consciousness as the soul looks upward into the face of Christ and outward to a broken world. Thus, the more a person grows into spiritual maturity, the more that believer's own sin and the Lord's forgiving grace stand out in bold relief. This is in sharp contrast with popular notions of growth and success, in which human progress is marked by self-promotion. The way of the cross is the road to true, final joy and fulfillment, but it's a path along which the maturing believer is stripped of all self-congratulation. The way of Christ is self-forgetting and God-exalting—a narrow road rejected by many, and yet it is the path to life (Matthew 7:13–14).

Preserving Necessary Paradoxes

The various tensions and paradoxes before us highlight the need to handle Scriptures wisely. Tunnel-vision treatment of Bible passages

and impatient "proof texting" lead to evading uncomfortable paradoxes, while the biblical calling is to embrace and proclaim "the whole
counsel of God" (Acts 20:27). Isolating a given teaching or command
from its context is sure to lead to error and the misapplication of
Scripture in the spiritual formation process.

For example, believers who latch onto Philippians 3 and become
restless, straining, striving disciples are at great risk of losing track of
God's all-important grace and peace; they fail to "be still, and know
that I am God." They're also in danger of a self-exalting mindset that
overvalues human effort in the larger process of "work[ing] out your
own salvation" (Philippians 2:12). By contrast, Christians who put
down roots in Philippians 4 without understanding the nuances are
at risk of twisting proper contentment into spiritually corrosive complacency—which, perhaps ironically, is also a self-exalting condition.
Further, not just individuals but Christian groups and congregations
can carelessly become either restful to a fault (even smug?) or excessively restless (agitated?). But the biblical calling to hold restlessness
and restfulness in tension remains essential for healthy spiritual life
and growth.

A key implication of the ideas in this chapter is that believers'
expectations about what spiritual progress "looks like" or "feels like"
can be badly off the biblical mark. No doubt we're tempted to take
in popular ideas of what constitutes a vibrant, healthy personal life.
In contemporary Western society personal growth is thought to be
marked by outward success (e.g., financial gain or social elevation),
and such developments are expected "in short order." Patience to
await the fruits of long, hard seasons of cultivating and pruning is not
a cultural value.

In fact, impatience is promoted—at times, implicitly—as an ideal.
Various tools of today's media feed demands for instant gratification
and discourage sustained reflection. The fiber-optic Internet connection I'm using as I write this book delivers data to my computer at

"blisteringly fast" and "mind-bending" speeds (to borrow from the company's ads). Mere text is peanuts for digital transmission. To send a copy of this book by e-mail attachment seems to take about two seconds. Downloads travel at speeds of up to 50 Mbps (megabits per second), and this means I can download ten songs in eight seconds or upload fifty high-resolution photos in twenty seconds. We love quick results! And yet, to complicate things, the widespread practice of multitasking and the corresponding waning capacity to engage in deep, demanding, thoughtful interaction don't bode well for serious spiritual formation, paradoxes included. Are today's busy believers prepared to grapple with the full range of God's ways of shepherding and shaping souls?[13]

The way forward for deliberate churches that desire earnest spiritual enrichment is, first and foremost, for the people to lift up their eyes and look upon the face of Christ. Paul connects progressive spiritual transformation with "beholding the glory of the Lord." "And we all, with unveiled face, beholding the glory of the Lord, are being transformed into the same image from one degree of glory to another. For this comes from the Lord who is the Spirit" (2 Corinthians 3:18). There's hope for defusing soul-deadening impatience when we gaze upon the Lord—he distracts us from silly toys and fleeting pleasures. There's hope for dislodging habits of mind-dulling multitasking when we gaze upon the beauty of God (Psalm 27:4). And there are great prospects for major advances in knowing and trusting God when we humbly accept his Word *as it is* and seek to embrace its fullness, rather than grasping at isolated texts or falling for careless religious sound bites.

---

13. See, e.g., Nicholas Carr, "Is Google Making Us Stupid?" (http://www.theatlantic. com/doc/200807/google); Walter Kirn, "The Autumn of the Multitaskers" (http://www. theatlantic.com/doc/200711/multitasking); and Mark Bauerlein, *The Dumbest Generation* (New York: Penguin, 2008) (cf. a review of Bauerlein: http://www.firstthings.com/ article.php3?id_article=6370).

It's not our calling to block out the Bible's paradoxes or somehow alleviate tensions it preserves. And it's not our job to fashion a spirituality with quick, feel-good benefits, for that would mean rejecting the maturation road on which we need time to take in both the enormity of our sin and the magnificence of God's grace. Fixing our eyes on Jesus is how God's children learn to live with joy and hope and endure the trials of this life, patiently resting in his secure love while eagerly pressing on to know and trust in Christ ever more and more (Hebrews 12:1–3).

When we set our heart's gaze on the glory and sufficiency of Christ, we can be content to walk through this present life as works in progress—souls under construction. We can be at peace with imperfect, unfinished lives because we know God is wise and good, and thus we accept his design for this age to include our gradual and not instantaneous spiritual renovation. After all, God can be trusted to bring to completion the good work he's begun in us (Philippians 1:6). And we can be content to live today *as sinners* (forgiven, growing, believing sinners who yearn for greater conformity to the image of God's Son), even though we engage continually in battle *against sin*.

Part Two

PRACTICAL APPLICATIONS

Chapter 7

A LIFE IN CONVERSATION WITH GOD

The way you enter into a conversation depends greatly on who the other person is. We speak differently with a telemarketing agent who calls during dinner than with the school principal or company CEO. Socialization involves learning the "rules" of interaction for a wide variety of settings. What do you say during a job interview? How about in a speech at a wedding reception? What do you say to the driver of the other car after a fender bender or to the police officer writing up the accident report? What do you say to an aging parent who can no longer live alone? The content of the conversation varies tremendously from one situation to another.

At the center of the Christian life is an ongoing conversation between God and his children. The Lord initiates this communication, speaking through his revealed Word, the Bible. God's written revelation is also accompanied by the witness of nature and the promptings of conscience (Psalm 19:1; Romans 1:19–20; 2:15). Further, the Holy Spirit's activity in the believer's life is vital (e.g., Romans 8:1–11).

But the Spirit's ministry surrounds and supports the witness of God's Word. As Jesus says in John 14:26, "The Helper, the Holy Spirit, whom the Father will send in my name, he will teach you all things and bring to your remembrance all that I have said to you." God's Spirit works in people's hearts and minds to make them receptive, clearing away resistance and preparing them to embrace the Bible's teachings.

Believers then reciprocate through prayer: God speaks, we respond, and the conversation goes forward. Prayer is much more than asking God for favors. It takes many forms, from jubilant praise to cries of sorrow, from heartfelt thanks to desperate pleas for help, from humble confession to bold appeals for life transformation. Even the very concise Lord's Prayer in Matthew 6 includes a variety of elements (see further below). So the conversational relationship believers have with the Lord is multifaceted and wide-ranging.

It's worth pausing to check our assumptions and get our bearings at this point and to remember exactly who the parties involved in this conversation are. It's not a discussion between equals. Let the "unevenness" of the divine-human interaction sink in. On the one hand, there's the eternal, glorious, all-powerful Maker and Master of the universe. On the other hand, there are humans—dependent creatures made in God's image but damaged through sin. We're needy and weak and prone to rebellion and foolishness. This is not a conversation between peers. In this chapter we look for ways to be alert to God's magnificence and our own ongoing, far-reaching brokenness as we interact with the Lord.

Indwelling Sin Interferes with Handling the Word of God

Indwelling sin causes intense, ongoing disruption to the conversation believers share with the Lord. In particular, it interferes with the way Christians receive and handle the Word of God, especially in the way we're inclined to favor some passages and ignore others.

If you find yourself in a crowded restaurant with loud background music, it can be hard to sustain a conversation—especially with someone who's not right beside you. Or if you are at a party with several conversations going on all at once, filling the room with a dull roar, it can be hard to compete with the noise and truly communicate with others. Of course, God is quite able to talk over other voices, and sometimes he asserts himself so as to be heard loud and clear. But often he chooses *not* to overwhelm us with his voice. Instead, he addresses the quiet heart, speaking in a still, small voice (1 Kings 19:12; Psalm 46:10). Further, in so doing he doesn't drown out all false teachings and distortions of his Word.

Given God's restraint in speaking to humanity and the various sin struggles every authentic Christian experiences, the stage is set for communication breakdowns. How is our handling of the Bible affected by seasons of slow growth and recurring defeat and by the harsh fact that we never truly "arrive" at a perfect understanding or application of the Word? Time is a friend in many ways, especially God's gracious gifts of second chances and time yet to repent and trust in Christ (2 Peter 3:8–9). But the lingering presence of remaining sin can be very disheartening. How does this impact the believer's use of the Bible?

A flowerbed "generates" weeds in short order if it's not cared for frequently. The best gardens receive daily attention to prevent such infestation. Think of the ways we misread the Bible as spiritual weeds. For example, when the Word confronts cherished habits, we're tempted to reinterpret a passage to dodge its clear message. The inclination of "the flesh" is to obscure or dismiss direct challenges issued by God, zeroing in instead on isolated words of comfort. Over time, believers who aren't humble and honest before the Lord's penetrating searchlight (Psalm 139:23–24) will create mental blind spots to insulate the soul from "those upsetting texts." The quest to embrace "the whole counsel of God" (Acts 20:27) must become a lifelong pursuit; one doesn't simply get over this hurdle and then carry on with discipleship—this task is at the very heart of the lifelong conversation with God.

At its root, dodging biblical teachings and lifting others out of context reveals a crisis of lordship. Who's in command? We may imagine this question is settled decisively at conversion or early in the Christian's spiritual walk, but in fact it keeps cropping up—that's what indwelling sin is all about. So, as we read (or preach) through books of the Bible and commands or warnings pop up here and there, we should always be on the lookout for sin reflexes that say, "Dodge this, feature that, ignore this, highlight that."

Of course, it's easy to point fingers when it comes to misusing the Bible. The sobering truth is that all believers need to see themselves as perennial learners in this area.[1] But that shouldn't keep us from identifying some glaring examples of this kind of Scripture twisting in action. I think of various "prosperity gospel" teachers and their selective readings of the Bible that dwell on the prospect of gain while avoiding texts that consider God's purposes in our losses.

Mac Hammond, pastor of Living Word Christian Center in Minnesota, declares repeatedly, "God wants you to be a winner in every area of life!"[2] This means winning at work, in relationships, and in the financial area. "God's highest and best is that your whole life becomes a reflection of His abundant provision."[3] However, this positive ideology leaves no room for God's freedom to work for good through suffering (see, e.g., Philippians 1:29; Hebrews 12:3–11). Further, muzzling the Bible this way leaves the believer defenseless when pain

---

1. D. A. Carson's *Exegetical Fallacies*, 2nd ed. (Grand Rapids: Baker, 1996) is an excellent aid for such learning. See also James Sire's *Scripture Twisting* (Downers Grove, IL: InterVarsity Press, 1980).

2. See materials from Mac Hammond at www.lwcc.org as well as www.mac-hammond.org.

3. *Winner's Way Magazine*, Fall 2008, 3 (http://magazine.mac-hammond.org/Main.php?MagID=1&MagNo=2).

strikes: "How dare God deny his children their royal entitlements?" It's a setup to find fault with the Lord.

Nigerian pastor Michael Okonkwo says God provides for his children to be wealthy here on earth: "When I say wealthy, I mean very, very rich. . . . Break loose! It is not a sin to desire to be wealthy."[4] Yet this counsel brazenly tramples Scripture: "But those who desire to be rich fall into temptation, into a snare, into many senseless and harmful desires that plunge people into ruin and destruction. For the love of money is a root of all kinds of evils" (1 Timothy 6:9–10).

Since 1999 Joel Osteen has pastored Lakewood Church in Houston, the largest church in North America. More recently he's become a best-selling author with *Your Best Life Now, Become a Better You,* and *It's Your Time.* Osteen's message applauds the power of positive thinking. "It's important that you program your mind for success."[5] If you believe "good things" are coming your way, they will. He repeatedly conceptualizes success and God's favor in terms of financial gain (e.g., elegant homes, increased salary, and business expansion). Osteen characterizes his own parents' preprosperity lifestyle this way: "They were good people, but nobody in our family had ever amounted to much. They lived under a curse of poverty and defeat."[6] The assessment of nonprosperous persons as never having "amounted to much" is deeply disturbing for how it measures human value in earthly terms.

The prosperity teachers blatantly exhibit a chronic tendency of all human hearts, namely, enlisting the Bible to reinforce our wishes while keeping God from meddling where we don't want him to go. But this posture cannot be sustained without a reckless or at least careless handling of the Word that mutes vast segments of it. The

---

4. Isaac Phiri and Joe Maxwell, "Gospel Riches," *Christianity Today* (July 2007): 23. See also John Piper's bold challenge to the prosperity teachers in *Let the Nations Be Glad!* 3rd ed (Grand Rapids: Baker, 2010), 15–32.
5. Joel Osteen, *Your Best Life Now* (New York: Time Warner, 2004), 13.
6. Ibid., 24.

fact that many professing Christians continue to flock to prosperity preachers year after year indicates that greed dies hard. In the end, religious people can get so confused that God's gifts become idols in place of the treasure that is God himself.

Strategies for Imperfect Believers to Handle God's Perfect Word

In light of the serious danger of misusing the Bible because of indwelling sin's damaging effects in our lives, what strategies can we adopt to minimize the harm? How can flawed disciples take steps toward a proper interpretation and application of the Scriptures? This has been a pivotal concern for the church through the ages; major controversies have revolved around how to understand the Bible's teaching. Our concern, however, is more tightly focused: what can we do to limit damage that indwelling sin causes to our conversation with the Lord when it comes to handling the Scriptures?

Paul instructed Timothy to scrutinize the way he used the Bible: "Do your best to present yourself to God as one approved, a worker who has no need to be ashamed, rightly handling the word of truth" (2 Timothy 2:15). Much is at stake here. It would be shameful to misuse God's Word; one would fail to be "approved" in the use of Scripture. The phrase "rightly handling" renders a Greek term for imparting something without deviation or dilution.[7] The text calls for straightforward, direct adherence to what's taught. By contrast, a latent tendency of the human heart is to bend the bold words of God, conveniently silencing some and emphasizing others.

To stay on target with the Word, a first and crucial step is to admit our self-serving tendency. Facing up to the disturbing reality that our hearts are corrupt and deceitful (Jeremiah 17:9) can be unsettling, even painful. The proud soul looks to steer around this difficult

---

7. See, e.g., Max Zerwick and Mary Grosvenor, *A Grammatical Analysis of the Greek New Testament* (Rome: Biblical Institute Press, 1981), 641 (*orthotomeō*).

admission: "I know my Bible. I understand its teaching. I wouldn't twist its message. I can trust my instincts when it comes to reading the Word." Reading with humility, however, doesn't mean acting like you never really know where you stand, but it does call for patience, an attitude of listening and learning, and an open mind to revisit and review one's interpretation of biblical texts through the stages of spiritual maturation.

It's also vital to grapple with the Word of God within the fellowship of the church. Many errors of personal idiosyncrasy and blind spots can be identified and corrected as the Bible is embraced within the body. Chapter 8 will look closely at the role of Christian community, but even here as we ponder strategies for handling the Word wisely, it's crucial to think corporately. This doesn't diminish the importance of individual and even private study. But wise believers will submit the fruits of their learning to the larger fellowship for consideration.

Further, studying the Scriptures within community should involve reaching out in various directions. Teachable Christians, for example, will want to learn how those of other spiritual traditions see certain biblical texts and related themes. The fact that a Presbyterian differs in some respects from a Pentecostal, or an Eastern Orthodox adherent from a Catholic, should not keep sincere believers from listening to and learning from those who stand in different "places." In addition, discerning believers will seek out the insights available from churches and godly leaders across cultural lines. The wider global church, for example, can learn much from the body of Christ in South Korea about following the New Testament call to mission and the charge to stand firm for Christ in a pressured environment.

Moreover, it's crucial to interact with movements of God's Spirit and reputable Christian leaders who've gone before us. Today's believers stand on the shoulders of generations of godly men and women who studied Scripture and wrestled with its proper application and who made major contributions to Christian learning and growth.

When I catch myself reading contemporary authors only, I make a point of reaching into the past to help get a fuller perspective.

Further, to limit the ill effects of indwelling sin, Bible interpreters need a mixture of humility and confidence. Humility is fitting since we can always learn more and since our sinful inclinations are always at work to distort the Bible's message. Further, the passing of time can create what we might call the "old shoe" effect: after a while you no longer notice ubiquitous features in the environment—it's the tourists who gaze up at skyscrapers, while New Yorkers don't pay attention to them. With time the custom of reading around difficult texts becomes second nature, and eventually we almost forget those hard words are still there. Oddly, then, as a believer matures, the passing of time generates new obstacles for responsible handling of the Bible. So one way new believers and younger Christians can encourage spiritual "veterans" is by helping them continue to see the parts of Scripture that may have become invisible over the years.

Humility needs to be held in a dynamic tension with confidence that God has communicated his truth to humanity in an intelligible way. It's a careless overreaction to step away from the Bible and say, "Hard to be sure what it really says. People have such different readings. Maybe it all boils down to your presuppositions." To be sure, the mood of many in today's postmodern milieu leans in this way. But a careful, honest reading of representative interpreters of the Word through the last two thousand years reveals a large field of clear, core teaching, and therefore it seems irresponsible to fall into any kind of despair about the accessibility of the Lord's message. God is great (and thus able to communicate with us) and God is good (and because of this he desires to communicate with us), and his Word comes to us in such a way that it can be grasped and obeyed, for the good of his people and the advance of his reign.

Indwelling Sin Disrupts the Life of Prayer

Ongoing sin is also disruptive and destructive to the life of prayer. Prayer is central to being equipped with the "armor of God" for battle with the Enemy (Ephesians 6:18–20), so if Christians can be kept from meaningful prayer—if they can be kept busy or distracted or downcast—then Satan has a major advantage, and believers are seriously vulnerable to his attacks. C. S. Lewis wisely points out that Satan's cause is never in greater danger than when Christians pray![8] So, of course, he'll fight back and do anything possible to disrupt, distract, and deflate praying Christians.

A common way prayer disintegrates is when it's reduced only to asking. Jesus teaches his people to ask, seek, and knock (Matthew 7:7–11), but in the big picture, in the Lord's Prayer and throughout Scripture, petitions are just one element. "Hallowing" the Father's name means praising him—declaring from the heart that God is glorious. Further, appealing for forgiveness implies confession of sin. An attitude of repentance and remorse must be evident when sincere believers, conscious of their many sins, come into the awesome presence of the Holy God through prayer. Thanksgiving is a widespread biblical motif that has a pivotal place in the believer's prayers (1 Thessalonians 5:18). In fact, it's hard to imagine how one's relationship with the Lord can be healthy and whole if gratitude isn't prominent in prayer.

Further, because of sin's confusion, believers often fall into a prayer pattern that limits requests to horizontal interests only. That is, we pray for temporal help (e.g., better health, secure jobs, safe travel) and yet are strangely silent when it comes to pleading with the Lord for spiritual gains in our own lives (e.g., for great strides forward in the mortification of sin) or the lives of others (e.g., for a loved one to see the folly of sin and recognize the beauty of Christ and joyfully run to the Lord for forgiveness and eternal life).

---

8. C. S. Lewis, *Screwtape Letters* (New York: Macmillan, 1961), 21.

This happens not only in the private prayers of believers but also in corporate petitions often lifted up in church gatherings. In my own ministry experience I see this tendency and feel its pull. Prayer time takes us through the requests for traveling mercies, successful surgeries, fruitful job searches, and the like—perfectly fitting prayer petitions. But the problem comes when they claim center stage in our conversation with the Lord. If we have little more to say than asking for creature comforts here and now, something is badly askew in our awareness of who God is and what it means to know him and be his children and be a part of spreading his glory among all the peoples of the world (Habakkuk 2:14; Matthew 28:18–20).

When we practice shrunken prayer (i.e., dwelling on requests and temporal comforts), it's no surprise that the vitality of conversation with God dries up. John Piper claims that prayer "malfunctions" when it's reduced to a domestic intercom on which we call up the butler to bring us some pillows. Instead, prayer is intended by God as a battlefield walkie-talkie used to call in life-saving soul reinforcements in the spiritual war being waged.[9] This kind of fervent, life-and-death prayer is rooted in a passionate commitment to God's reign and the spread of his fame. It's much easier, frankly, to fall back into small prayers to a small God who's interested in little more than soothing us when we face earthly pressures. Then indwelling sin takes strategic advantage of our feeble hearts and prompts us to view small-minded petition as "normal."

When it comes to prayer and petition, another difficulty confronts believers, and it becomes more intense as time passes. The problem is that we expect results on a certain timetable. If we've prayed for a year for someone to get a job, we wonder if something's wrong—wrong with God or with his leading or goodness or with the person we're praying for. After all, what possible reason could there be for, say,

---

9. John Piper, *Let the Nations Be Glad!* 3rd ed. (Grand Rapids: Baker, 2010), 69–70.

remaining unemployed a whole year? Or what if we appeal for healing and our ailing loved one doesn't improve—or even declines and eventually dies? And then, on a spiritual wavelength, what about when we pray for an unsaved friend or relative? What are we to think when we watch our loved one go on year after year dismissing or defying Jesus Christ? How do we understand prayer requests to which God apparently says no?

God weaves prayer and waiting together in the experience of his people. Texts linking petition with expected results don't set a time frame. God may grant the healing, but *when* will our dear friend be healthy and whole? Will it be on a schedule that, humanly speaking, would seem like a quick result? Will it come only after extended waiting? Or will it occur only in the age to come? Jesus' repeated teaching on persistence in prayer (see Luke 11:5–8; 18:1–8) implies that waiting is a regular experience for his disciples, even if it isn't always the rule. In waiting we can begin to practice faith; without waiting, it's hard to know what it would mean to trust the Lord for anything. In his book *Waiting*, Ben Patterson points out that "at least as important as the things we wait for is the work God wants to do in us as we wait."[10]

But with waiting, various facets of sin's lingering ugliness can also rise up in believers' hearts and interfere with the prayer conversation. Time gradually erodes the niceness we wear on the surface, and a deeper self-serving inclination seeps out. In turn, the ego-based outlook results in being irked that God doesn't give us what we want within a "reasonable" amount of time. Patience is a fruit of the Spirit that's often in short supply. Large doses of waiting may bring out a contentious or defiant spirit in the hearts of still-maturing believers.

The passing of long seasons also makes prayer vulnerable to sloppy caricatures and harmful stereotyping. For example, we get used to

---

10. Ben Patterson, *Waiting* (Downers Grove, IL: InterVarsity Press, 1989), 11.

prayer forms (including times and places, bodily positions, overused phrases, and predictable requests) and can inadvertently latch onto such externals, losing track of the essential heart transaction true prayer involves. In this way prayer gradually becomes beige and uninspiring. And from there it's a short step to valuing just the maintenance of prayer forms, whether they express rich relational substance or not.

Our sinful inclination is to degenerate into formal and shallow prayers. And yet, Jesus is very clear in denouncing the type of spiritual life that's mere routine: "This people honors me with their lips, but their heart is far from me" (Matthew 15:8). When professing believers go through prayer's motions while their hearts are elsewhere, a grievous affront to the Lord is committed. It's as if we lose track of who God is and what it means to be given an audience before the Master of the Universe.

Would we yawn and doodle while sitting face to face with Hollywood stars or our sports heroes? I doubt it. And yet, honesty compels me to admit there have been many times my mind has wandered in prayer even while my body and voice have carried on in robotic fashion—a kind of mental multitasking before His Majesty. This is a type of temporary spiritual insanity. If it weren't for the grace of God, of course, such profane disrespect for his magnificence would merit severe wrath. How thankful we as praying people should be for the mercies of the Lord that are new every morning (Lamentations 3:23)!

At the same time, if we're running headlong into deliberate sin, we can't count on prayer as a technique to tidy up our mess. To willingly run after sin's pleasures, imagining we can always "play the prayer card," is to misunderstand what it means to believe in God. First of all, Hebrews 10:26 sternly warns against brazen sin: harboring sin and giving oneself over to it erode the soul and undermine the heart's capacity to turn back to God.

And second, numerous texts of Scripture indicate that our prayers hit the ceiling and fall flat on the floor if we're nurturing sin and remain unrepentant: Husbands who act sinfully and don't honor their wives find their prayers "hindered" (1 Peter 3:7). Calling on God with sinful motives results in receiving nothing (James 4:3). Authentic prayer begins when a heart is humbled, aroused by God's splendor, and moved to sincere confession and faith. But prayer games by willful sinners are mere noise.

Strategies for Imperfect Believers to Meet God in Prayer

As with handling God's Word, when it comes to prayer we need strategies as well to limit and potentially counteract the destructive impact of our lingering sinful nature. Prayer is a vital means of growing in grace;[11] it's a primary way we resist the Devil and draw near to God (James 4:7–8). The words of Jesus to his disciples in the garden of Gethsemane are apt: "And when he came to the place, he said to them, 'Pray that you may not enter into temptation.'" (Luke 22:40). Prayer is a critical, God-appointed means of resisting enticements to sin. John Owen puts it this way: "Whoever wishes to avoid temptation must pray. . . . If we do not abide in prayer, we will abide in temptation."[12]

Effective strategies for meeting God in prayer invariably require Christians to come face to face with their deep spiritual wickedness. This is distressing and unsettling. We're stripped of our self-assurance and ego-centered righteousness and left spiritually naked before the Lord. Within the fellowship of believers, then, it's not hard to imagine that true spiritual openness and honesty involve painful self-disclosure.

---

11. J. I. Packer, *Faithfulness and Holiness: The Witness of J. C. Ryle* (Wheaton: Crossway, 2002), 195–97; John Owen, *Sin and Temptation: The Challenge to Personal Godliness*, Classics of Faith and Devotion, James M. Houston, ed. (Portland: Multnomah, 1983), 44–47.

12. John Owen, *Sin and Temptation*, 124.

But we resist allowing others to see us as feeble, needy, and depraved, even though there simply is no way forward in spiritual maturation apart from laying down our arms, admitting we have no leverage with God, and laying bare our sinful souls.

This is why ongoing confession has to be central in spiritual maturation. We need to establish regular patterns of individual and corporate confession.[13] "Therefore, confess your sins to one another and pray for one another, that you may be healed" (James 5:16). "If we say we have no sin, we deceive ourselves, and the truth is not in us. If we confess our sins, he is faithful and just to forgive us our sins and to cleanse us from all unrighteousness" (1 John 1:8–9). Of course, as mentioned above, praying, "Forgive us our debts," is an implicit confession of sin.

It may be painful to admit that our hearts are prone to wander and bent toward magnifying ourselves rather than the One worthy of all praise. But there's no way ahead into spiritual health and growth apart from this humbling self-recognition. In fact, the practice of earnest prayer itself heightens our awareness of sin and the need to confess.[14] The great psalms of confession (32 and 51) provide vital and impassioned wording for such cries from the believing sinner's heart: "Have mercy on me, O God, according to your steadfast love; according to your abundant mercy blot out my transgressions. Wash me thoroughly from my iniquity, and cleanse me from my sin! . . . Create in me a clean heart, O God, and renew a right spirit within me" (Psalm 51:1–2, 10).

To be sure, there's always the risk that confession will become a mere habit, a mindless ritual rehearsing the appropriate words of contrition. This can and does happen, for example, in both liturgical and nonliturgical churches. The use of either prepared prayers or

---

13. Anthony A. Hoekema, *The Christian Looks at Himself* (Grand Rapids: Eerdmans, 1975), 60.
14. John Owen, *Sin and Temptation*, 46.

spontaneous confessions can degenerate into stock phrases that roll off the tongue, pass over the ears, and yet fail to register in the heart. One way to limit this inevitable challenge is to make some use of both prewritten prayers and spontaneous utterances; the variation can help the sincere believer remain alert.

Another risk of incorporating confession into prayer practices is that people may mistakenly assume the act of confession is a necessary human performance in order to hold on to a slippery salvation. There's a key distinction to maintain here. A real spiritual event takes place when confession is made. In 1 John 1:9 it's described as being forgiven and cleansed. The vision of Psalm 51 is that confession leads to the restoration of joy and mobilizing for active witness. But the gift of salvation simply is not presented in Scripture as tenuous or temporary, such that one would be repeatedly "re-earning" the new birth. The importance of ongoing confession, rather, is to express faith in Christ by admitting sin, giving thanks for saving and sanctifying grace, and conveying one's longing for interpersonal closeness in the vital, moment-by-moment walk of spiritual communion with the Lord that is threatened by unconfessed sin.

Since time can put prayers under pressure (e.g., about where God is or why he hasn't apparently acted), the battle for spiritual maturation will mean seeking a wise biblical balance of strong hope and humble receptivity. The Bible contains many examples of answered prayer, such as the famous victory of Elijah over the prophets of Baal (1 Kings 18:36–39), as well as injunctions to call on God in faith and expectation (Matthew 7:7–11; James 1:5–8; 5:13–16). Further, God is certainly able to grant the healing or employment (etc.) his people plead for (e.g., Genesis 18:14; Psalm 115:3; Jeremiah 27:5; Mark 9:23; Ephesians 3:20–21), so there's every reason to be confident that, if he sees fit, he'll certainly provide the desired blessing.

But this kind of unwavering hope should be balanced with a humble openness to God's good and wise ways, even when our wishes aren't granted.[15] Job fell into an attitude of contending with the Lord (Job 40:1–9), but he also had moments of spectacular faith. Following the tragic death of his ten children, Job announced, "The LORD gave, and the LORD has taken away; blessed be the name of the LORD." At least at that stage of the narrative, he walked in faith and didn't charge God with any wrongdoing (1:21–22).

Persecution is a common theme in the New Testament. Peter tells believers not to be surprised when it comes (1 Peter 4:12). Praying for protection is right and good, but God does not always provide it. Hebrews 11 tells of believers who won victories by faith (11:1–34) and who were martyred by faith (11:35–38). The apostle Paul pleaded with the Lord for relief from his "thorn . . . in the flesh," but God said no (2 Corinthians 12:7–10).[16] When James and Peter were arrested by Herod (Acts 12), James was executed but Peter spared—and eventually Peter was released from prison by a miracle in conjunction with prayer made on his behalf (12:5–17). Are we to assume that no prayer was made for James? In the end, a fair handling of the whole Bible brings to a dead halt any demanding approach in prayer. Instead, maturation means remaining humbly open to God's ways and his answers to our appeals, even if those answers clash with our wishes.

In addition, a strategy for drawing near to God despite the pressures of indwelling sin is to pray in partnership with Christian brothers and sisters. As with handling the Word of God, we benefit by carrying on much of our conversation with the Lord in the fellowship of the body. It's crucial, then, to build shared prayer into our expectations of church life. We need each other's involvement and support as we fight to sustain this practice that the Enemy is eager to ruin.

---

15. M. Craig Barnes (*Yearning: Living between How It Is and How It Ought to Be* [Downers Grove, IL: InterVarsity Press, 1992], 80) confronts the reduction of prayer to a tool that "works." The only prayer that always works is when God's people ask him to hold their broken lives in his arms of grace. Most of the time, that has to be enough. Prayer as an act of being in God's presence is an end in itself.

16. See further chap. 11 on God's good purposes in the trials of his people, even those afflictions resulting from others' or their own sins.

The church I serve has a traditional midweek prayer meeting, which I lead, and that circle of brothers and sisters has become a sweet center of spiritual encouragement. I don't know how many times we've come together, dashing in from dinner or work or the most recent round of chemotherapy, only to see the Lord grab hold of our anxious hearts through his Word and grant his peace as we meet him in prayer. One person is out of work, again. Another friend is at a loss for how to love adult children whose lives are in disarray. We share and pray, and we part with a sense of God's consolation that we don't carry our burdens alone.

Unfortunately, however, it's all too easy for believers to rub shoulders and fail to enter into deep communion with God together. Perfunctory prayers to introduce meetings or official prayers by pastors don't constitute a corporate culture in which people keep up on each other's spiritual needs and practice joint prayer (e.g., as pairs, in small groups, in classes). Wise church leaders will teach from the Word and give practical guidance on building the members' relationships around prayer. A praying fellowship, in which there's a strong commitment to love, patience, and confidentiality, is an environment where shared holiness thrives.

Of course, many factors work against that caliber of spiritual community life, such as the mobility mindset (people move in and out of churches "with the greatest of ease"). Spiritual maturation is closely tied to a willingness to commit and remain deeply involved in fellow believers' lives, despite the challenges and disappointments that crop up in the body. Another prayer deterrent is an activist mindset that measures a person's worth by his or her deeds. Against that notion come sage words from the International Day of Prayer for the Persecuted Church organizers: "The least you can do is the most you can do—pray."[17] This slogan reflects the biblical truth that God's

---

17. See http://www.persecutedchurch.org.

power far exceeds our strength. And it's in prayer that we show we believe this.

Spiritual Disciplines and the Conversation with God

Deploying various spiritual disciplines is also important for the divine-human conversation. Richard Foster has helped lead a resurgence of appreciation for the disciplines in recent decades, especially through his well-known book *Celebration of Discipline*.[18] He speaks of three categories of disciplines: inward, outward, and corporate. We'll say more on the corporate life in chapter 8. And Foster's outward disciplines (simplicity, solitude, submission, and service) are, for the most part, practices grounded in and inspired by the inward disciplines (meditation, prayer, fasting, and study). It's these inward, or we might say "vertical," disciplines that we'll consider briefly here. Speaking of them as vertical helps us be more explicit about the attention to God and communion with God that are pivotal in the right exercise of spiritual disciplines.

Foster corrects various misunderstandings at the outset.[19] The word "discipline" may have connotations of drudgery and severity, but the practices in view actually offer a way to break through destructive habits and open a door to joy in God's presence. The idea that the disciplines are a way of flexing human willpower is also a gross distortion. In fact, practicing the disciplines is a way to exercise faith and hope. They're a gift from God: "The Disciplines allow us to place ourselves before God so that he can transform us."[20] Further, Foster's comments on the historic practices of spiritual formation remind us

---

18. See also Dallas Willard, *The Spirit of the Disciplines* (San Francisco: Harper and Row, 1988).

19. Foster, *Celebration of Discipline: The Path to Spiritual Growth*, 2nd ed. (San Francisco: Harper and Row, 1988), 2–7.

20. Ibid., 7.

that the disciplines aren't recent innovations but ancient means of seeking God that have sometimes been neglected.

Pursuing a wide range of disciplines helps believers not to fall into a narrow spiritual practice in which prayer and Bible reading are rigid, routine acts that allow the devotional life to become monotonous. For example, we not only study the Bible, but also meditate on it[21]—mull it over, digest its life-sustaining message. Meditation is a practice that's realistic about our distracted lives and the need to become quiet and calm in the Lord's presence. As such, it's a practice in which prayer and our experience in the Word overlap.

Further, prayer goes beyond language. We can also pray with our bodies—and fasting is one such gesture.[22] Fasting is a kind of prayer in which we "say" to God, using body language, that we long for his presence and working in our lives more than we long for our next meal.[23] Practicing the spiritual disciplines expands our "vocabulary" for interaction with God and enriches our experience of resting in his presence. Donald Whitney gives a helpful caution: fasting without a purpose "can be a miserable, self-centered experience."[24] By contrast, fasting for strategic reasons can contribute to deep spiritual growth. Among the positive purposes for fasting are the following: to strengthen prayer, seek God's guidance, express grief or repentance, battle against temptation, and worship the God we desire above all else.[25]

---

21. In some respects it seems Foster's chapter on meditation (chap. 2) isn't adequately focused on God's Word, yet he does make this statement: "For all the devotional masters the *meditatio Scripturarum*, the meditation upon Scripture, is the central reference point by which all other forms of meditation are kept in proper perspective."
22. Gestures such as kneeling or lifting hands also have meaning.
23. John Piper, *A Hunger for God: Desiring God through Fasting and Prayer* (Wheaton: Crossway, 1997), 90, 96.
24. Donald Whitney, *Spiritual Disciplines for the Christian Life* (Colorado Springs: Nav-Press, 1991), 165.
25. Ibid., 165–78.

Humility and Hope

God's intention is that we'd be profoundly changed by spending time in his presence through Scripture and prayer. The deepening of our communion with the Lord is always possible in light of his power and love. But such vital hope should be held in tandem with a humility that leaves the shaping of our conversation in God's hands. Our understanding of his Word can be flawed, and our aspirations in prayer can be misguided. Further, expectations we bring to the vertical conversation may be off the mark. For example, if we suppose that advancing in our apprehension of the Word and the life of prayer will come easily, or naturally, or without times of confusion or bewilderment, then we're guilty of wishful thinking. The fact remains, it's within God's wise and sovereign design for the present age that his people would both make great strides in drawing close to him (and so, be hopeful), yet also recognize their serious shortcomings in the vertical relationship (thus inspiring a greater longing to revel in God's joyous presence).

Chapter 8

MATURING IN AND AS COMMUNITY

An old African proverb says, "If you want to go fast, go alone; if you want to go far, go together." Quick-fix approaches to spiritual life driven by impatience and animated by bursts of energy can bring about impressive outward effects, but do they last? Without diminishing the importance of individual believers' personal faith, all too often Christians fail to see the vital place of growing together in corporate discipleship. The body of Christ needs the spiritual contribution of each member, and each member needs the support of the body.

In J. R. R. Tolkien's epic tale, *The Lord of the Rings,* a long and desperately difficult trek is attempted by a fellowship of nine. When attack and betrayal disrupt the team, two unspectacular characters end up taking the ominous "ring of power" to destroy it in the fires of Mount Doom in the distant land of Mordor. Frodo and Sam are hobbits, small but sturdy, and the duty falls to them. Frodo bears the burden, and his trusted friend Sam is at his side through thick and thin. As their arduous journey unfolds, one potential peril after another strikes (e.g., the massive spider Shelob, or their off-and-on companion, Gollum, who feigns loyalty to get his hands on the ring). Frodo finally collapses in a heap near spewing lava on the slopes of Mount Doom—he can't go on. Faithful Sam pleads with Frodo to get up, but it's no use. Then Sam says, "Come, Mr. Frodo . . . I can't carry it for you, but I can carry you and it as well. So up you get! Come on, Mr. Frodo, dear! Sam will give you a ride."[1] And so Sam hoists his friend right to the mouth of the cave where the ring is finally destroyed.

True Christian fellowship is similar: our journey can be very trying, but we travel together and carry each other when the load is too great. In this chapter we'll probe deeply into spiritual formation in and as a Christian community. Our focus is the dynamic of church life—and by "church" here I envision not only traditional congregations but also ministry teams, fellowship groups, and various types of Christian communities that are part of the larger body of Christ.

The Foundation of Personal Faith

Before going further, it's important to clarify that the personal faith of individual believers is the essential footing of authentic Christian community. For example, John 3:16 declares, "For God so loved the world, that he gave his only Son, that whoever believes in him should not perish but have eternal life." Here believing is an action of individuals. "Whoever believes" is singular; the Greek expression could also be translated "the one who believes."

Romans 10:9 summarizes the essential spiritual response to Jesus this way: "If you confess with your mouth that Jesus is Lord and believe in your heart that God raised him from the dead, you will be saved." Modern English doesn't allow us to differentiate between singular and plural forms of "you," but Greek does, and in Romans

---

1. J. R. R. Tolkien, *The Return of the King* (New York: Del Rey Books, 1993), 233.

10:9 each instance of "you/your" is singular. And so, people aren't saved as a result of merely being associated with others who have faith in Christ. Numerous similar statements in the New Testament make it explicit that saving trust in Jesus Christ is rooted in the hearts of individuals.

Insisting on the necessity of personal faith, of course, doesn't mean salvation is a private matter. Further, in some cultures individual action is very much linked to the will of the community and especially to the direction of key leaders such as a family father or village elders. The vital point here, however, is that even if a group or community makes a positive response to Christ together, to be genuine that faith needs to extend to and be the experience of individual believers. A corporate Christianity that doesn't rest on the foundation of the personal faith of particular people lacks authenticity.

There are many critiques of Western individualism and the ways it has distorted spiritual life into a solo performance, a "Lone Ranger" endeavor of isolated and private believers. We do well to hear such warnings. Western individualist values often clash with the church's body life. But some critics go too far, diminishing and virtually dismissing personal faith. Katharine Jefferts Schori, the presiding bishop of the Episcopal Church, denounces "the great Western heresy—that we can be saved as individuals, that any of us alone can be in right relationship with God."[2] The grain of truth here is that, as members of the body of Christ, we need each other. But it's badly misleading to speak of individual salvation as "heresy"; personal faith in Christ is central to the Bible's teaching on God's redemptive work.

Paul David Tripp is more cautious in his critique of individualism: "Under the influence of Western culture, Christianity tends to take on

---

2. Katharine Jefferts Schori, "Opening Address at General Convention 2009" (http://www.episcopalchurch.org/78703_112035_ENG_HTM.htm). See also the response of Richard J. Mouw, "The Heresy of 'Individualism'?" *Christianity Today* (July 2009), web-only edition, www.christianitytoday.com.

a uniquely individualistic cast, a 'Jesus and me' kind of faith. We talk much about a 'personal relationship with Jesus.' And it is certainly true that we are brought, by God's grace, into personal communion with Christ. But Christianity is equally a faith that is meant to be anchored in community."[3] This description keeps the personal and corporate dimensions of spiritual life in balance, as is necessary in any effort to be faithful to Scripture.

John Bunyan's classic allegory, *The Pilgrim's Progress,* narrates many twists and turns in the trek to the Celestial City during which the protagonist, Christian, gains support from fellow travelers. In one scene, Christian and Faithful arrive at the town of "Vanity Fair," where anything and everything is for sale (one must pass through Vanity Fair to get to the Celestial City). Though minding their own business, Christian and Faithful are mocked, falsely accused of causing bedlam in the city, beaten repeatedly, and thrown into prison. As followers of Jesus, they don't seek to retaliate, and this remarkable display of grace wins over a few of the town's more thoughtful onlookers. But it only infuriates the rabble, and they call for the death of Christian and Faithful. In the midst of this madness, the two men comfort each other, reminding one another that if this is the end, it's a quick transport to the Celestial City. And so, they uphold each other during the darkest trials, urging one another to be faithful unto death. As the story unfolds, Faithful is executed in Vanity Fair, but Christian escapes— and journeys on in the company of a new friend, Hopeful. Spiritual camaraderie is a pivotal theme in Bunyan's poignant allegory.

Interdependence within the Body

Various New Testament passages compare fellowship within the church to the interdependence among the parts of a human body. This

---

3. Paul David Tripp, *Broken-Down House: Living Productively in a World Gone Bad* (Wapwallopen, PA: Shepherd Press, 2009), 153.

is developed most fully in 1 Corinthians 12, where the unity *and* diversity of believers within the body of Christ are highlighted.[4] Initially the accent falls strongly on the unique giftedness of each person; even though there's only one Spirit, there are varieties of gifts (e.g., wisdom, knowledge, faith, healing, miracles, prophecy, discernment, tongues, and interpretation). In 1 Corinthians 12:12–13, however, attention turns to the oneness of the church: "For just as the body is one and has many members, and all the members of the body, though many, are one body, so it is with Christ. For in one Spirit we were all baptized into one body—Jews or Greeks, slaves or free—and all were made to drink of one Spirit."

Here's the key concept: widely diverse members together form one body in which the whole needs the parts just as the parts need the whole—and as this is true of a physical body, so it is with the body of Christ, the church. Paul then asks several rhetorical questions that press the comparison. How foolish would it be for the foot to say, "Because I am not a hand, I do not belong to the body," or the ear to say, "Because I am not an eye, I do not belong to the body"? Paul then asks the Corinthians to imagine the absurd: "If the whole body were an eye, where would be the sense of hearing?" Imagine a solitary eyeball—no socket, no head or hands or feet attached! The reader begins to see how outrageous it would be for members of the body of Christ to be at odds with or isolated from one another. Unity and diversity must be kept in a healthy balance: "As it is, there are many parts, yet one body. . . . Now you are the body of Christ and individually members of it" (12:20, 27).

The Christian community is a spiritual organism in which sincere followers of Jesus Christ can grow and thrive. Separation from other

---

4. In addition to 1 Cor. 12:12–31, see also Rom. 12:4–5; Eph. 1:23; 4:4, 12–16; 5:23, 30; Col. 1:18, 24. Paul David Tripp (*Instruments in the Redeemer's Hands* [Phillipsburg, NJ: Presbyterian and Reformed, 2002], 327) asserts that it's impossible to think of sanctification as an individual concern in light of 1 Cor. 12 and Eph. 4.

Christians, or even a lifestyle of casual or shallow friendships with other believers, doesn't match the vital, day-to-day interdependence God desires for his people as they make the heavenward trek together.[5] Let's go back to physiology. Think how often the eye needs the hands or feet to move the body or to take some action, and think how often the other body parts need the eye to spot some danger or opportunity.

The analogy from the human body shows how God situates his people in a deep and dynamic fellowship—something more than ordinary friendship. A vital and vibrant body life in the church, in which all members give and take, bless and receive blessing, "Rejoice with those who rejoice, weep with those who weep" (Romans 12:15)—a community life of this caliber is the Lord's "new normal" for Christ-followers venturing together in this life. That kind of close and countercultural fellowship, of course, can make observers sit up and take notice: "By this all people will know that you are my disciples, if you have love for one another" (John 13:35).

Rich and Karla are devoted followers of Jesus, and their home has become a magnet for young people searching for answers as well as acceptance. You might call their place a spiritual "safe house," a refuge in a threatening world. I see the traffic jam around their driveway; the flow of friends in and out of their home is constant. Karla and Rich themselves don't always recognize it, but it's no surprise to believers who know them: the love of Jesus is shared by them and their family, and it becomes a beacon of hope beckoning the weary to come in.

Jesus' prayer for future generations of disciples in John 17 takes this further: "I do not ask for these only, but also for those who will believe in me through their word, that they may all be one, just as you, Father, are in me, and I in you, that they also may be in us, so that the world may believe that you have sent me. The glory that you have given me I have given to them, that they may be one even as we are

---

5. Paul David Tripp (*Broken-Down House*, 152) warns against "terminally casual relationships," noting, "We live with the delusion that we know each other, but we really don't."

one, I in them and you in me, that they may become perfectly one, so that the world may know that you sent me and loved them even as you loved me" (17:20–23). The prayer and passion of Christ for his church is oneness, and oneness of a quality akin to the perfect unity shared by God the Father and God the Son! That is a breathtaking vision. Of course, then, this isn't a grit-your-teeth-and-get-along oneness, or a mere hi-in-the-hallway unity. The model is the lofty, joyous, loving oneness within the Godhead.

Why does Jesus pray for this? Of course, the sheer delight of being unified under the smile of God is itself a purpose for the church to function this way. But there's more: "so that the world may believe" that the Father sent the Son (17:21). A unified church is a public-relations victory for the gospel. Believers living in humble, peaceable unity underscore the core message of God's love for humans. To put it the other way around, the world scorns and mocks a divided church as a people who have nothing to say—nothing unbelievers aren't already painfully aware of through their own broken, divided lives.

Perhaps all of this talk of oneness might sound rather idealistic. But if we bear in mind that Paul writes to the Corinthians about healthy unity in diversity precisely because of their sad, sharp divisions (e.g., 1 Corinthians 1:12; 3:4), we get a more realistic picture. Further, since all believers continue to battle with sin all their lives, the body of Christ must be recognized as a spiritual organism made up *entirely* of flawed members. In Christ we're forgiven, and in Christ we're under construction and (hopefully) making some advances against the temptations of sin. But the fact remains that the body of Christ is a community of sinners, and when sinners live together in close fellowship, there's trouble.

Measures for Mutual Ministry

We can take the body analogy further and consider sickness. How do the members of a human body impact one another when disease strikes? And what would it mean to live with illness affecting every body part, every organ, every system—digestive, cardiovascular, nervous, muscular, skeletal, and others? After all, in the church all members are broken sinners who are far from fully "healthy" in Christlike holiness. How would a person's physical health be affected if disease were pervasive in this way?

To refine the picture, we should bear in mind that the degree of sickness varies from believer to believer—some being well along the way in the pursuit of God and corresponding spiritual formation, yet others being "back in the pack" or even lagging far behind. Returning to physiology, it's as if certain ailments were minor, even if chronic (like recurring athlete's foot or poor vision), while other maladies were more serious and had the potential for devastating damage to the whole body (perhaps high cholesterol or even malignant cells). In the church, then, how do we support each other knowing that all givers and recipients of care are ailing and realizing that some are relatively healthy while others may be deathly ill? Several measures are in order.

First, we need to seek God's help to break through any proud resistance to seeing *ourselves* as unwell and in need of ongoing grace—as lifelong sinners, the walking wounded, who are bound to cause damage within the body. Alcoholics Anonymous wisely makes this number one of its twelve steps toward recovery: "We admitted we were powerless over alcohol—that our lives had become unmanageable."[6] Similarly, in the church there must be a genuine coming to terms with the fact that we're all sick. And this isn't just for individuals; facing the facts is the first step in moving toward corporate health.

Second, and following closely, church bodies must cultivate an attitude of shared humility. A humble spirit is vital if one is going to be molded into conformity with the image of Christ (Romans 8:29). It is

---

6. http://www.aa.org/pdf/products/p-55_twelvestepsillustrated.pdf.

a process of ongoing breaking and rebreaking, shaping and reshaping, and one must be pliable; defensiveness obstructs progress in holiness. Leaders need to work hard to demonstrate and communicate that it's normal and urgent for people to receive correction and to live together in ways that are outward looking rather than self-focused. Further, when God's people recognize a kind and humble spirit in the lives of their leaders, many barriers to spiritual maturation in the body are removed.

Third, it's urgent for church bodies that seek spiritual wellness to keep their focus on God's Word. The Bible is our handbook for health in the church; it's God's message of how we can advance against sin and temptation. Think of the Scriptures as God's prescription for well-being in the body—follow the Doctor's orders in order to get better! And, by contrast, think of the spiritual messages of leaders who don't diligently expound the Word of God as prescriptions for disease and misery.

A fourth vital step in supporting and serving each other in the body of Christ, in light of our illness, is to be patient in seeking and receiving God's healing touch. Sanctification is a lifelong process, and many of the changes that God's Spirit brings about among his people are gradual. Progress definitely can be made in this life; the Lord is active in the lives of his people, helping them to "work out" (i.e., live out) their salvation in God-honoring ways (Philippians 2:12–13). So believers should be hopeful people—hopeful yet patient.

Fifth, God's people need to learn practical skills to address corporate sin problems. For example, believers could be trained to apply biblical principles of conflict resolution. Ken Sande's book *The Peacemaker: A Biblical Guide to Resolving Personal Conflict* is a fine tool for this purpose.[7] In addition, Christians need to be involved in

---

7. Ken Sande, *The Peacemaker: A Biblical Guide to Resolving Personal Conflict*, 2nd ed. (Grand Rapids: Baker, 2003). See also the many helpful resources available through www.peacemaker.net.

mentoring relationships so they, in turn, can help fashion the body life of believers in Christlike ways. The Navigators have a long legacy of discipleship ministry, and they've produced numerous useful tools.[8] Further, belonging to an accountability group is another way to offer mutual support in the battle against sin in ways that cannot be done in larger gatherings. It can be helpful to establish a set of questions that all group members answer when they meet, probing questions that ask a person to reveal how he or she is doing in the fight against particular sins.

Caring for "One Another"

The Greek pronoun translated "one another" occurs a hundred times in the New Testament, and in many instances in texts instructing believers how to treat each other. "One another" calls for reciprocal action—two-way ministry, giving *and* receiving support. Carrying out the various one-another commands of the New Testament requires settings and forums in which give-and-take ministry can occur (such as small groups). In a sense, then, I am "my brother's keeper."[9] We don't go it alone. Here are several representative one-another passages:[10]

- Show hospitality to one another (1 Peter 4:9)
- Accept one another (Romans 15:7)
- Be subject to one another (Ephesians 5:21)
- Bear with one another (Ephesians 4:2)
- Forgive one another (Colossians 3:13)
- Confess your sins to one another (James 5:16)
- Pray for one another (James 5:16)

---

8. See the various materials available at www.navigators.org.

9. This should not be pressed to the point of trying to "fix" someone else or falling into codependent patterns of protecting and propping up others rather than helping them learn to stand on their own two feet. There is sometimes a fine line between loving care and careless enabling.

10. See also the "one another verses" in James C. Wilhoit, *Spiritual Formation as if the Church Mattered*, 154–55.

- Encourage one another (1 Thessalonians 4:18)
- Confront one another (Colossians 3:16)
- Stir up one another (Hebrews 10:24)
- Be kind to one another (Ephesians 4:32)
- Honor one another (Romans 12:10)
- Bear one another's burdens (Galatians 6:2)
- Love one another (Romans 13:8)

Confess Your Sins to One Another

We'll focus attention on a few of these commands that are especially related to dealing with sin in the church. James 5:16 says, "Therefore confess your sins to each other and pray for each other so that you may be healed. The prayer of a righteous man is powerful and effective" (NIV). It's fitting, as well, to confess our sins before God—following the Lord's Prayer effectively does this ("Forgive us our debts"). But James 5:16 calls for horizontal confession—and not merely to a priest or pastoral figure, but in a reciprocal fashion, to "one another." All members of the body need to give and receive confessions; all are at fault and need to admit it, and all are victims of others' sinful acts and thus have the opportunity to reflect the grace of God by extending kindness to the offender.

Richard Foster observes that confession is difficult because we view the believing community as a fellowship of saints more than as a fellowship of sinners. We imagine that others are far ahead of us in terms of spiritual progress, so we don't want to admit our failures, and instead we hide the truth, acting as hypocrites.[11] But if we truly recognize God's people as a fellowship of sinners, we're freed to make our confessions. It's crucial to keep in balance (and in a certain dynamic tension) the Christian's Bible-based identity as both sinner and child of grace.[12]

---

11. Richard Foster, *Celebration of Discipline*, 145.
12. Paul David Tripp, *Broken-Down House*, 35–43.

Consider the experience of Ray Boltz, a Christian musician who's come out of the closet and announced he's gay.[13] Mike Ensley wonders whether the church let Boltz down by not being the kind of community within which he could reveal his struggles and get help to follow God's Word: "So, as much as I sympathize with a Church that grieves the lost perception of a cultural hero, I sympathize all the more with a man who has been forced to struggle in secret for decades by the very community he served." "Forced" may be too strong a term, but Ensley's observation that the church can seem to be an unsafe place to be honest about our sin struggles must be taken to heart.

The "got it all together" image many Christians try to project is dishonest. And it does damage by preventing hurting, broken seekers from seeing the church as a welcoming community. Further, it invites scorn from the general public, which senses that Christians aren't as perfect as they'd like to be.[14] Two key principles of Christian community are support and sanctification—and in that order, says Mark McMinn. Loving support comes first, as is demonstrated by the wide-open arms of the father receiving his prodigal son home after a season of vile sin (Luke 15:11–32).[15] It may be an oversimplification to separate support and sanctification this way, but it's surely true that support must not be withheld from those who still have a long way to go in the practice of holiness.

Larry Crabb rightly warns against the sinner's self-protectiveness that keeps others at arm's length—it's a silent killer of community. In the church this serious ailment can show itself in friendliness, humor, efficiency, shyness, and other ways.[16] Craig Barnes helpfully points to the relief that comes when we break through such fears: "When you

---

13. Mike Ensley, "Ray Boltz's Hunger for Community" (http://www.boundless. org/2005/articles/a0001918.cfm).

14. On this point, see further my article "Impractical Christianity," 80–82.

15. Mark McMinn, *Why Sin Matters: The Surprising Relationship between Our Sin and God's Grace* (Wheaton: Tyndale, 2004), 175.

16. Larry Crabb, *Inside Out*, 100.

have finally found the courage to tell someone the truth about your guilt, the last thing you want to hear is that you're not so bad. What you want to hear, what you have to hear, is that you are forgiven. It's the only way you are going to get back on your feet."[17]

Taking James 5:16 seriously *requires* us to open our hearts to trusted fellow believers. Secret sin is toxic; there's wisdom in the adage "You're as sick as your secrets." But sometimes professing believers hide their sins because, deep down, they love their reputation more than they love Christ and they're unwilling to endure the humiliation of honest self-disclosure.[18] Further, Christians may conceal secret sins because they suppose others will reject them if they open up. However, very often when one believer is daring enough to speak out about a personal sin struggle, others will quickly and thankfully step up and acknowledge they too face such a battle.

A wave of revival poured over many Christian colleges in 1995, and with it came special gatherings of corporate worship, prayer, and confession.[19] Students would line up for hours on end to confess their sin openly. Tears of relief were met by gestures of love from fellow disciples who were also seeking God's forgiveness and renewing grace. I appreciate Norm Wakefield's observation that sin thrives in secrecy, so hiding sin only allows its grip to grow stronger. Sin prospers where guilt, shame, and worthlessness are stressed. But he goes on to give hope: "When there is openness, sin loses its power to manipulate and control us."[20]

---

17. M. Craig Barnes, *Searching for Home,* 91. In *Messy Spirituality: God's Annoying Love for Imperfect People* (Grand Rapids: Zondervan, 2001), Mike Yaconelli states, "When you and I stop pretending, we expose the pretending of everyone else. The bubble of the perfect Christian life is burst, and we all must face the reality of our brokenness" (27).
18. Tim Chester, *You Can Change,* 123–24.
19. For an account of the 1995 revival at Wheaton College, see http://www.wheaton.edu/bgc/archives/revive.html.
20. Norm Wakefield, *Who Gives a R.I.P. about Sin?* (Downers Grove, IL: InterVarsity Press, 2002), 128.

To be sure, in some circumstances revealing one's secret sins would indeed lead to rejection or other serious hardships. Such harsh treatment could come to an honest believer when others lack the humility or maturity to deal with such confession, and so they might sever ties with or lash out against the broken sinner. Or painful consequences could follow simply because the discovery of grave secret sins would disqualify one from a position of spiritual leadership or would deeply damage cherished relationships (how many stories could be told of marriages and families ruined in this way?[21]). But regardless of anticipated painful results, the message of James 5:16 is clear and still stands: confess your sins to one another.

Encourage One Another

The practice of encouraging one another is also an urgent form of mutual ministry for sinful believers. Two texts in Hebrews merit special attention, one of which is 3:12–14: "Take care, brothers, lest there be in any of you an evil, unbelieving heart, leading you to fall away from the living God. But exhort one another every day, as long as it is called 'today,' that none of you may be hardened by the deceitfulness of sin. For we have come to share in Christ, if indeed we hold our original confidence firm to the end." First there's a warning: Watch out for an evil, unbelieving heart in any individual within the fellowship. Keep an eye on each other's hearts (of course, the text assumes the existence of open relationships with meaningful sharing). This is crucial because such a heart could lead someone, eventually, to turn away from God.

What precautionary measure can be taken to fight this danger? Encourage one another. Build each other up in faith and hope and help each other trust the living, reigning God. And do so *daily*. Such

---

21. Strictly speaking, the ruining of such relationships shouldn't be tied so much to the disclosing of secret sin, but to the sin itself. Sin can't be harbored in one's heart without bringing damage not only to the sinning individual but also to those with whom that person's life intersects.

ongoing spiritual support is intended by the Lord as a key way to keep people from being hardened in sin.

Is it necessary to keep our faith in Christ intact through life's trials and to the end? Verse 14 clearly says that it is. And perseverance is a community project. That is, it's not just up to me to take care of my heart, nor is it your solitary task to look after your own faith. We are to encourage each other in ways that go far beyond nice platitudes and words of cheer. The church is intended to be a community of deep support and faith-building, sin-confronting, grace-extending encouragement. But this isn't natural—by nature we complain and see the glass half empty, and we drag each other down. By nature we see the sin in our brother or sister and point fingers and fire stinging darts (or if we're less bold, we at least console ourselves self-righteously that we're not so bad).

The other text in Hebrews is 10:24–25: "And let us consider how to stir up one another to love and good works, not neglecting to meet together, as is the habit of some, but encouraging one another, and all the more as you see the Day drawing near." Here mutual encouragement is paired with the ministry of "stirring one another up to love and good works." This helps us discern the nature of biblical encouragement: more than just conveying right information, it stimulates fellow believers to practice God-honoring actions. Encouragement is practical; it arouses believers to live as they intend to and ought to live while following Jesus together.

An interesting problem of the church(es) addressed in Hebrews surfaces here, namely, the tendency to neglect meeting together—to be sluggish or careless about getting face to face with each other on a regular basis (remember "every day" in 3:13 or "daily" NIV). In our day a thousand distractions and "good activities" interfere with regular gatherings of believers. No longer does Western culture prop up church programming by keeping Sunday morning free from alternative activities. Many today see church involvement as one more enrichment option to be considered at a smorgasbord of choices. Many believers have fallen right into this danger (some unknowingly, to be sure), lowering their commitment to the body of Christ and elevating the importance of all kinds of alternatives. As a result, church participation by many who profess heartfelt faith in Christ has become more and more erratic.

The risk taken in letting anything get in the way of consistent mutual ministry within the body life of the church is serious: it means the loss of opportunities to give and receive spiritual encouragement, and that, in turn, means spiritual threats of the most serious kind (see Hebrews 3:12–14). Today more than ever, amid distracted lives, church leaders must be bold in helping their people resist the spiritual decline and demise that can come from inconsistent gathering and irregular encouragement. We simply were not designed to stand up and endure in our faith without giving and receiving deep spiritual encouragement on a very regular basis.

Ironically, some worship songs can undermine the spreading of Christian encouragement. Music that speaks of devotion to the Lord in simple or absolute terms may leave worshipers with a nagging sense that they don't measure up or that such songs are out of touch with reality. Further, lyrics of radical, unflinching allegiance may leave God's people feeling that their praises are dishonest—we know ourselves too well. Songwriters who paint an overly lofty picture of the Christian life[22] thus invite unnecessary discouragement, even if their intention is to do just the opposite.

Simplistic songs that declare how believers definitively give over to Christ every shred of their being misconstrue the biblical message: God's reign has dawned, but the full light of noonday will only appear

---

22. E.g., "You're Worthy of My Praise," by David Ruis, which makes blanket promises of faith and obedience and praise to the Lord with the totality of one's being, but fails to reckon with the lingering work of facing and fighting sin. Or consider "You Are My King," by Billy Foote; do we truly glorify God in all our actions?

in glory. To be sure, our aim and desire is to grow in faith and advance in zeal for God's honor. We seek his help to obey, and we long for the day of perfect praise in the very presence of Christ. But this side of heaven the battle goes on. Discerning songwriters incorporate admissions of weakness and cries for aid along with declarations of praise and dedication.[23]

In order to avoid unneeded discouragement, believers should treat lofty lyrics of grand devotion as words of hope; such perfect union with and honor for the Lord are certainly our vision and longing, and they will be fully attained in glory. And it can be achieved in part, in rich and profound ways, even now as we grow in Christ and journey on together, encouraging and building one another up.

Bear with One Another

Paul teaches believers to bear with one another: "I therefore, a prisoner for the Lord, urge you to walk in a manner worthy of the calling to which you have been called, with all humility and gentleness, with patience, bearing with one another in love, eager to maintain the unity of the Spirit in the bond of peace" (Ephesians 4:1–3). "Bearing with" renders a Greek verb (*anechomai*) meaning "to endure, put up with." So it's not a flattering depiction; no one likes to think that others must "bear with" his or her presence in the Christian community. Of course, it's a two-way street, and humility means being ready to bear with and care for *one another.*

---

23. E.g., Marie Barnett's "Breathe," which is a cry of desperation for the Lord's life-giving presence. Or Ben Fielding and Reuben Morgan's "Mighty to Save," a song applauding God's saving mercy and acknowledging our faults and sins. From an earlier era (1772), consider William Cowper's hymn "O for a Closer Walk with God," expressing zeal for Christ amid the fierce battle with sin: "I hate the sins that made Thee mourn, And drove Thee from my breast." Cowper goes on to confess to idolatry: "The dearest idol I have known, Whate'er that idol be, Help me to tear it from Thy throne, And worship only Thee."

And when we come across someone who is, shall we say, "difficult," our calling is to bear with the person *in love*. And love is characterized by seeking what is in another's best interest. It would be unwise to treat this command, however, as an excuse for allowing someone to wallow in sin rather than helping that person seek change. ("Well, we're taught to just put up with him.") The point is not to endure any and every kind of problem that arises, but to love and accept people even as efforts are made to help them grow in faith and obedience to Christ.

Confront One Another

Colossians 3:16 commands believers to confront one another: "Let the word of Christ dwell in you richly, teaching and admonishing one another in all wisdom, singing psalms and hymns and spiritual songs, with thankfulness in your hearts to God." To admonish is to confront and correct. The reluctance to admonish (driven perhaps by fear of rejection) is a failure to love. Of course, correcting others is always a delicate matter, since we may be mistaken or we ourselves may be in greater need of correction. It's always wise to examine one's own heart and conduct first, making sure that any rebuke is received personally before looking at others (Psalm 139:23–24; Matthew 7:5).

Bear One Another's Burdens

The image of Sam carrying Frodo up the slopes of Mount Doom comes back to mind when considering the charge to bear one another's burdens: "Brothers, if anyone is caught in any transgression, you who are spiritual should restore him in a spirit of gentleness. Keep watch on yourself, lest you too be tempted. Bear one another's burdens, and so fulfill the law of Christ" (Galatians 6:1–2).

We need to address a few major features of this important passage on handling sin within the body. First, what does it mean to be "caught" in a transgression? Does Paul have in mind a culpable sinner (as when someone is caught with his or her hand in the cookie jar) or the unsuspecting soul caught off guard by sudden temptation and inadvertently swept up into transgression?

For several reasons, the former option is best: We should avoid letting transgressors off the hook by saying that sin "caught" and compelled them to disobey the Lord. It's "transgression" in which one is caught, and the transgressing of God's standards is not presented as something believers slip into innocently in Paul's letters (or in the New Testament generally). Rather, "transgression" is a culpable act (e.g., Matthew 6:14–15; Romans 5:15, 20).

Second, the warning to watch out in case "you too be tempted" (Galatians 6:1; see also 1 Corinthians 10:12) implies that the person who has been caught in transgression got there via a wrong response to temptation—he or she succumbed to sin's enticement. Third, even though the Greek verb translated "caught" (*prolambanō*) is passive here (i.e., the person doesn't catch something but is caught), the word doesn't carry a moral connotation in and of itself. That is, the use of this verb doesn't favor either innocence or culpability on the part of the one caught. In light of this, it's best to let "transgression" and "temptation" in the immediate context prompt us to assign fault to the transgressor in view—the person has consciously disobeyed the Lord.

And yet, such a person in the church is not to be judged or rejected or excommunicated, but rather "restored." Believers scandalized by the sins of their brothers and sisters may be tempted to judge them. But after transgressing God's commands, the primary need is for the faltering believer to be returned to a clear and close fellowship with the Lord—to be reconciled to God. This is similar to what's in view in the Lord's Prayer with "forgive us our debts." It's not that Christians are getting saved and resaved over and over, but rather that the spiritual air is being cleared and that impediments that stain the relationship are being washed away.

A secondary, horizontal restoration would then involve reintroducing the transgressor back into the life of the church and rebuilding relationships that may have been broken through the sinful episode. Such restoration might involve a person's returning to his or her prior stature and role within the body (though perhaps only after some time), or it might require a significant process of "recovery" and retraining in which a believer never resumes previous responsibilities.[24] The crucial matter is the transgressor's being embraced and loved by the body of Christ with a view to gaining victory over sin and walking in harmony with the family of believers.

Such care for fallen Christians is a crucial way to "bear one another's burdens" (Galatians 6:2). The two-way "one another" means next time it could be you who's caught in sin and needs others' help for spiritual victory and restoration. We also bear each other's burdens when we, for example, pray for each other or assist in times of illness or crisis (e.g., by helping care for children or providing meals or giving rides). But the thrust of Galatians 6:1–2 must not be missed: reciprocal burden bearing also includes working to rescue each other from the grip of sin. This means being open and transparent with each other even when it feels uncomfortable. It may mean walking with one another in places we'd rather not go. In a Christ-centered church we can go to our leaders for support in what may prove to be dark waters.

We mustn't miss the imagery of our passage that sin has a way of "catching" believers—it has tentacles. The dynamic of evil is that the more one chooses to step into it, the more entangled one gets. Sin entraps. The morning after a church picnic, I stumbled upon a paper cup half full of lemonade that had been missed during the postfestivity

---

24. On the question of whether a pastor should return to the pastoral ministry after a moral failure, see, e.g., R. Kent Hughes and John H. Armstrong, "Why Adulterous Pastors Should Not Be Restored," *Christianity Today* (Apr. 3, 1995): 33–36; and Kenneth S. Kantzer, "The Road to Restoration: How Should the Church Treat Its Fallen Leaders?" *Christianity Today* (Nov. 20, 1987): 19–23.

cleanup. Apparently in the insect world the word got out that treasure had been found—they'd won the lottery! Scores upon scores of ants and spiders and other bugs made their way up the side and over the rim and down into a pool of sugary bliss. Trouble is, once in the compelling brew, they couldn't get out, and the next day revealed a grim picture of dead bugs floating in their chosen pleasure. Sin entangles believers in self-destructive habits, and we get stuck. Galatians 6:1–2 teaches that being caught in sin is something from which one needs the help of others to break free; once submerged, you can't just climb out on your own.[25] Strong churches will be proactive in looking for and pursuing their people who get caught in the Enemy's traps.

Forgive One Another

The command to "forgive one another" is essential to the health of the body: "Put on then, as God's chosen ones, holy and beloved, compassionate hearts, kindness, humility, meekness, and patience, bearing with one another and, if one has a complaint against another, forgiving each other; as the Lord has forgiven you, so you also must forgive" (Colossians 3:12–13). Here again believers are taught to "bear with one another." Even though Paul also has a lofty vision of the church's identity (cf. Ephesians 3:10; 5:25), there's a brutal realism about body life as well. The harsh fact of our sins and weaknesses means we bring more "cold pricklies" and fewer "warm fuzzies" to the community than we may care to admit. We're living in denial if we don't expect interpersonal adversity within our heaven-bound convoy.

God gives us a model for conduct within his church, namely, the action of his Son. On the eve of his arrest, Jesus washes the disciples' feet, an example of how they were to serve each other as he had served them. Then he tells them they were to love one another as he'd loved them (John 13). In Philippians 2 Paul calls on Christians to relate to each other with the self-giving disposition of Christ. And here in

25. Larry Crabb, *Inside Out*, 156.

Colossians 3:13 believers who have grounds for making complaints against each other are taught to forgive. "As the Lord has forgiven you, so you also must forgive"—not mere advice, but an urgent command.

What does forgiving actually entail? To be clear, it does not mean pretending the offense never happened, nor does it mean that the offender should face no consequences for his or her misconduct. Forgiving someone does not imply that a disrupted relationship can suddenly be "rewound" to where it was in terms of interpersonal affection and trust prior to the wrongdoing. Even in the best of circumstances, rebuilding trust can take a long time.

By contrast, forgiving means refusing to retaliate (vengeance is God's business) and refusing to hold others' sins against them. And more than that, positively it involves sincerely desiring and seeking God's best for the offending party (love for enemies would want nothing less). Further, forgiving others is not to be conditional upon their making a change for the better. We simply must forgive; it's an essential effect of knowing and trusting God (Matthew 6:12, 14–15). When believers are vividly conscious of all that they've been forgiven by the Lord (Luke 7:47), they grow in readiness to imitate and extend that forgiveness to their flawed brothers and sisters.

Maturation of Communities

So far in this chapter, we've focused on how individuals treat (or should treat) each other within the church fellowship. We've looked at how each member needs and is needed by all others in the body, and we've probed into several "one another" commands to see what is taught about the nature of God-honoring reciprocal ministry. But going further, how can the maturity *of a church* be discerned? What does it mean to "grow up" as a spiritual fellowship?

Culture is sometimes defined as the patterned way of doing things together. Within the web of relationships and customs and expectations and unwritten rules that exist in any church, a patterned way of doing things together is formed—a church culture. As with whole societies or any other groupings of humans, however, facets of a culture can become invisible to its own members. This is because practices often stem from reflexes and unstated assumptions.

Over the last few decades, blue denim has become the "required" look for casual clothing within Western culture. People feel the pull to conform to the blue denim rule. But, of course, it could be a different fabric or color. We think blue jeans are "right," but one can quickly point to other cultures where the common ideal is entirely different. The fact is, our customs settle into the realm of implicit values and unstated expectations. And that makes it hard to pinpoint them and evaluate their merits. When it comes to fabric, not much is at stake in terms of spiritual life. But there are other customs and expectations that take root in Christian communities that have major implications—positive or negative—for corporate maturation. We'll seek to evaluate such communal experience in light of Scripture.

One way to approach this is by tracking the literature on the key marks of a healthy church. In *The Purpose Driven Church*, Rick Warren distills from Scripture generally and from the Great Commandment (Matthew 22:37–40) and Great Commission (Matthew 28:19–20) in particular five tasks that Christ ordained for his church to accomplish: worship, ministry, evangelism, fellowship, and discipleship.[26] Warren's case rests on the basic and important assumption that churches can't mature if they aren't seeking to be the kinds of communities that the Bible teaches that they should be.

Ray Ortlund, drawing from John 15 and 17, boils it down to three priorities (he also speaks of three loves) for any strong local church: Christ, the body of Christ, and the world.[27] And the logical

---

26. Rick Warren, *The Purpose Driven Church* (Grand Rapids: Zondervan, 1995), 103–6.
27. Ray Ortlund, *Three Priorities for a Strong Local Church* (Waco, TX: Word, 1988), 19–20. Along similar lines, one could speak of three goals for the church: worship, nurture, and outreach (or "upreach, inreach, outreach," or "exaltation, edification, evangelism"). Edmund Clowney (*The Church* [Downers Grove, IL: InterVarsity Press, 1995],

ordering of these three commitments is important: "Where a church or group is not first vertical, first rich in God, it will be thin and poor in its horizontal relationships. And when it is not a deeply, spiritually united team, exploits for God in the world will come very hard. . . . Yet these priorities must be active all at once, and all the time."[28] The church that stays focused on these three areas will spare itself from getting caught up in many unnecessary schemes and programs, and it will stay on track with what's eternally important.

Zeroing in on these three priorities is an attempt to be concise yet also comprehensive. James Wilhoit hones in even more closely, settling on a single calling for the church: "Spiritual formation is *the* task of the church. Period."[29] Wilhoit quickly acknowledges that the church's calling includes witness, worship, teaching, and compassion. But he steps back to the Great Commission and its fundamental charge to make disciples, noting that believers must be "formed" more and more into the likeness of Christ in order to accomplish witness, worship, teaching, and compassion.[30]

The key question for us is this: are such marks characteristic of a church's leadership and body life, and are they widely accepted and valued within the culture of a congregation? The absence of such traits, or the lack of broad support for them among the people, would indicate a great need for progress in corporate maturation.

---

117) has essentially the same view: "The church is called to serve God in three ways: to serve him directly in *worship*; to serve the saints in *nurture*; and to serve the world in *witness*" (italics original).

28. Ortlund, 118.

29. James C. Wilhoit, *Spiritual Formation as if the Church Mattered*, 15.

30. Ibid., 15–16, 23. Moving in the opposite direction, other authors list numerous key aims of the church. Christian Schwarz names eight essential qualities in *Natural Church Development: A Guide to Eight Essential Qualities of Healthy Churches* (Carol Stream, IL: ChurchSmart Resources, 1996). Mark Dever names nine Scripture-centered marks of strong churches in *Nine Marks of a Healthy Church* (Wheaton: Crossway, 2004) cf. www.9marks.org.

Questioning Community Life

When seeking to assess a spiritual community's level of collective spiritual growth, I find it helpful to ask questions related to the key purposes of the church:

- Regarding worship and the vertical life: Is it evident that people are moved by the reality of God and impressed by his magnificence? Listening in on conversations will help reveal whether the wonders of the Lord are in the forefront of people's minds or not. Is the living, reigning Christ honored, admired, and "applauded" when people talk to each other, or would such comments come across as odd or even fanatical? Is there a sense of awe at the saving work of God through the death and resurrection of his Son? Is there a yearning for the return of Christ (Hebrews 9:28)? Square one of corporate spiritual growth is a shared sense of wonder at the character, revelation, and saving work of God.

- Regarding the Word and prayer: Is it common for people to "huddle up" and pray spontaneously, as needs arise? Is there a widespread sense that prayer not only is right but also has value—that being in God's presence has inherent worth, and depending on God's power is more effective than any other kind of "work"? Do people's prayer requests reach far beyond temporal creature comforts and show a deep yearning to revel in God's presence and see the advance of his reign? Do petitions express a peaceful sense of freedom to leave prayer's results in God's hands? Is the Bible treated as a reliable and relevant message on which to build every facet of church life? Is preaching clearly "bibliocentric," and are people eager to confirm in their Bibles the message that's proclaimed? Is the use of much time and energy for study of the Word widely affirmed?

- Regarding worship music: Does the repertoire of songs make room for humble, reverent worship that comes to terms with ongoing sin? Or do festive songs that oversimplify new life and spiritual transformation dominate the people's mindset? Do the songs of the community speak honestly, in keeping with Scripture, of authentic devotion and the need of daily mercies?

- Regarding perception of sin: Is there a widespread readiness to admit sin and express remorse over it? Does a survey of the conversations, activities, hopes, and dreams characteristic of a church body reveal a healthy fear of sin, along with a drive to join in battle against sin? Or, are some sins swept under the rug, or even ignored? ("It isn't hurting anybody.") Do people feel a need to appear like everything in their life is "just fine"? Is it socially off limits to confront certain sins? When sins are ranked and "less important" ones are overlooked, that's a signal of shared immaturity.

- Regarding practical service: Do people's convictions translate into concrete actions? Is it common to see prayer requests paired with plans to serve and support those who are hurting? Is it natural for Bible studies to spin off ministry projects? Is the congregation characterized by a sense of compassion and a vivid awareness of the struggles of people in its local vicinity, and does such lead to practical gestures of love and witness? When words of truth consistently fuel loving deeds, healthy growth is happening.

- Regarding flexibility: Is there an attitude in the air that reveres "the good old days," a love of the past, and an attachment to tradition? Do people assume that spiritual maturity can be measured by the number of years they've been believers? Or, by contrast, is there a reckless disregard for the church's roots and history and instead a love of all things new and different? In just about any church you can find individuals at either of these extremes, but if widely shared values within a Christian community swing to one pole or the other, it's a sign of stunted growth. In maturing fellowships believers will learn from the past and hold firmly to unchanging biblical truth, and at the same time they'll be eager to innovate in ways that help communicate the gospel to a changing world.[31]

- Regarding open communication: Does a church have a "past" that's off limits? Are there episodes in its heritage that no one seems to really know about—or be willing to talk about? Is there some kind of corporate pressure felt to portray the church in a certain idealistic light? Are there secrets about the congregation's imperfections that are too painful for people to talk about? Does the atmosphere of the fellowship seem brittle or excessively careful? Is there an "elephant in the room" that no one will name?

Peter Scazzero astutely points out how emotional health and spiritual health are inseparable—and he's not just talking about individuals. It's impossible for a congregation to become spiritually mature while remaining emotionally immature.[32] When supposedly mature believers are allowed to act (and continue to act) in unloving, defensive, insecure, unteachable, critical, conflict-avoiding, and passive-aggressive ways, red flags go up to identify an unwell church.[33] He adds that the links between individual and community are crucial:

---

31. Spiritual formation necessarily involves growth, and growth means change (not change of everything and not change for change's sake). So churches that are maturing will be churches receptive to prayerfully considered changes—even dramatic changes.
32. Peter Scazzero, *The Emotionally Healthy Church: A Strategy for Discipleship That Actually Changes Lives* (Grand Rapids: Zondervan, 2003), 50.
33. Ibid., 50–51.

"As go the leaders, so goes the church."[34] The starting point for change in the church is always the leader, and yet this process can be difficult and drawn out (e.g., it can involve digging into a pastor's family-of-origin dynamics, past struggles, and patterns of relating). Scazzero speaks to pastors: "We cannot grow an emotionally healthy church if we ourselves are not addressing issues beneath the surface of our lives."[35]

My church background is in the Baptist General Conference (more recently known as "Converge Worldwide"), and a hallmark of the BGC has long been its peaceable ethos. In fact, when speaking at the denomination's 2000 Annual Meeting, Luis Palau, in an effort to clarify what kind of Baptist group we were, said, "Now, you're the gentle Baptists—not the fighting type—right?" Of course, many other church groups might be characterized similarly, and a priority on peace certainly has its merits.

But overvaluing peacemaking can lead to peace faking.[36] A craving for peace at all costs actually delegates power to anyone, including the unfit, who might hold the system hostage by disruptive conduct in order to get their way. A maturing church community needs leaders and other key members who have the strength to pursue peace, but who do so without compromising the truth or losing their nerve under pressure from strident and contentious members of the body.[37] But more than that, a healthy, maturing Christian community will be one in which the broad majority of the people support their leaders,

---

34. Ibid., 36.
35. Ibid., 46.
36. I appreciate Ken Sande's distinction between "peace-making" and "peace-faking" (*The Peacemaker*, 22–23). Just being nice, smiling, and looking the other way—that's not the making of true peace. Real peacemaking involves honest, humble examination of conduct by people who are willing to admit fault and pursue change.
37. Cf. my paper presented to at the 2001 Annual Meeting of the Evangelical Theological Society: "Democracy, Codependency and the Irenic Spirit: Searching for the Boundaries of Implicit Theology in Evangelical Churches" (available at http://sinandspiritualformation.blogspot.com).

and those leaders work for peace but also advance the truth so that the body isn't held captive to peace at all costs.

The literature on codependency can provide another helpful window for considering corporate well-being.[38] Much has been written (especially in response to the struggles of adult children of alcoholics) on family systems and the dynamic of addiction to relationships and the need to please or cover for the mistakes of others—that is, codependency. Within a family, or any social system (such as a church family), when some members exhibit compulsive behaviors, others tend to come forward with reactive conduct, and these reactions end up enabling further harmful action by those with compulsive practices. Maturation progresses as reactive reflexes are brought under control within a Christian fellowship.

Leaving Church

These issues of peacekeeping and codependency often surface when people decide to leave a community of believers. When members walk away from "the family," it can create a painful crisis. Indeed, the deeper the relationships, the greater the trauma. In some ways it could be compared to the rift of divorce. Our question is this: how does a maturing body of believers "handle" the departure of members?

In our consumer culture, people often view church life in terms of shopping: "If it's not 'meeting my needs,' I'll go elsewhere; there's plenty of competition for my business."[39] I won't elaborate on how this attitude itself reveals a serious lack of understanding of what it means to be members of Christ's body, and I'll focus instead on how a community of believers might process this kind of difficult development.

---

38. See, e.g., Melody Beattie, *Codependent No More*. 2nd ed. (Center City, MN: Hazelden, 1992).

39. Cf. Michael Mangis, *Signature Sins: Taming Our Wayward Hearts* (Downers Grove, IL: InterVarsity Press, 2008), 221, on consumerism and church shopping.

First, in a healthy church there's a general awareness that some-times people do leave. Disappointing as this may be, the key concern is to see them join another fellowship where they can serve and be blessed. A maturing congregation doesn't allow its own loss to cloud the sky so fully that it can't look outward, prayerfully wishing depart-ing brothers and sisters God's best.

Second, when possible, it's valuable to keep in touch and speak openly with those who depart about their decision to leave. I've gained numerous helpful insights by meeting with people after they've left the church in which I was serving. (Sometimes the lesson has simply been that they didn't "fit," while in other situations serious flaws and failings came to light and could be addressed in the aftermath.)

Third, and primarily, even while we try to learn from the loss, it's critical to trust the Lord with the lives of his people and the composi-tion of his church. A human-centered, numbers-driven, anxiety-based approach to body life will surely lead to devastation when people sever themselves from our Christian communities, but faith in God oper-ates differently. We do well to remember that it's Christ who builds his church and that only the work of God is truly enduring (Matthew 16:18; Psalm 127:1). A given local church or Christian fellowship isn't *mine*: it's formed through the gracious, sovereign work of the One who gives and also takes away. Regardless of gains or losses, maturing church bodies can say, "Blessed be the name of the LORD" (Job 1:21).

We can also look at leaving church from the viewpoint of those exiting. Disillusionment with, for example, traditional "church ser-vices," one-way communication, property ownership (i.e., costs and hassles), and a church's perceived cultural irrelevance have led to the exodus of many. Such dismay has also helped fuel the house church movement and otherwise drive some believers toward a more flexible, decentralized body life.[40]

---

40. See, e.g., Julia Duin, *Quitting Church* (Grand Rapids: Baker, 2008); Frank Viola and George Barna, *Pagan Christianity* (Ventura, CA: Barna Books, 2007); Brian Sand-

Although it's impossible here to delve deeply into such issues, two basic observations are apt. First, all criticisms of churches should be taken to heart with humble receptivity. Even if some amount of exaggeration surfaces in the debate, growing believers and maturing fellowships will want to benefit from constructive criticism and the grain of truth it brings.

Second, Kevin DeYoung makes the valid point that some efforts to sidestep the "institutional church" and "organized religion" are naive. He asserts that the biblical and historical marks of the church necessitate a measure of structure and "institutionalization." "The church needs to regularly gather in worship, in prayer, to hear God's Word, and to receive the sacraments. It should be an ordered body where there's membership, leadership, and discipline."[41]

A key benefit of such organizational commitments, in fact, is helping God's people battle against sin and pursue holiness. Moving on to greener pastures after spotting flaws in the people and patterns of a given congregation closes the door to such gains. While "moving on" may be appropriate in the case of extreme failings, a wise general rule would be to keep seeking Christ together with one's family of imperfect brothers and sisters through thick and thin, adapting structures as needed, thus supporting one another in long-term spiritual formation.

Life Together

In 1933 Dietrich Bonhoeffer, a German pastor, delivered a speech over the radio in Berlin in which he rebuked the German public for turning to a leader who would become a "misleader" and even an

---

ers, *Life after Church* (Downers Grove, IL: InterVarsity Press, 2007).
41. In Katie Galli, "Why Churchless Christianity Doesn't Work: Kevin DeYoung Defends the Institutional Church," http://www.ctlibrary.com/ct/2009/august/35.58.html. See also Katie Galli, "Dear Disillusioned Generation," *Christianity Today* (April 2008): 69–70; Kevin DeYoung and Ted Kluck, *Why We Love the Church* (Chicago: Moody, 2009).

idol to them. The broadcast was cut off before he finished.[42] In that moment Pastor Bonhoeffer realized he'd have to go underground if he wanted to carry on in ministry, for he wouldn't have any part in the "German-Christian" compromise with the Nazis. In 1935 he accepted a call to take charge of an illegal, clandestine seminary where he lived together with twenty-five students undercover. It was there in 1938 that Bonhoeffer wrote *Life Together*, the story of rich and sweet fellowship in Christian community. He gives counsel on what it means to live as the church, to support your brothers and sisters in times of trial, and to know the joy of spiritual camaraderie. Bonhoeffer asserts, "It is not simply to be taken for granted that the Christian has the privilege of living among other Christians. . . . The physical presence of other Christians is a source of incomparable joy and strength to the believer."[43]

The testimony of believers under pressure amounts to a wake-up call for the church at large: spiritual camaraderie has immense value, and it mustn't be taken for granted. It's the privilege of God's people to seek his grace to help shape church communities, over time, into maturing, joy-giving, hope-stirring fellowships. Other relationships are precious too, of course (e.g., biological bonds or ethnic ties), but there's nothing like the church—the unique spiritual organism formed by Christ and made up of those who trust in him as they venture together.[44] The Lord is generous to give his people "one another" under his gracious headship.

---

42. Dietrich Bonhoeffer, *Life Together* (New York: Harper and Row, 1954), 10.
43. Ibid., 17, 19.
44. Cf. Rodney Stark, *Families at the Crossroads* (Downers Grove, IL: InterVarsity Press, 1993), 67–88, on "the church as first family"—the church and not the family is God's most important institution on earth.

Chapter 9

DEVELOPING IMPERFECT LEADERS

John Newton, the former slave trader who came to faith in Christ and served as an Anglican minister from 1764 until his death in 1807 (and also the author of "Amazing Grace"), once mused about the ingredients to make a perfect pastor:

> In my imagination, I sometimes fancy I could make a perfect minister. I take the eloquence of ____, the knowledge of ____, the zeal of ____, and the pastoral meekness, tenderness, and piety of ____; then putting them all together into one man, I say to myself, *this* would be a perfect minister. Now there is one, who, if he chose it, could actually *do* this, but he never did—he has seen fit to do otherwise, and to divide these gifts to every man severally as he will.[1]

---

1. Richard Cecil, *Memoirs of the Rev. John Newton* (London: William Baynes and Son, 1824), 106 (cited by John Piper: http://www.desiringgod.org/Blog/1926_why_there_are_no_perfect_pastors).

In fact, every pastor and Christian leader is a chronic sinner. I don't say this to point fingers or arouse despair, but simply to acknowledge the facts. Like all other followers of Jesus Christ, pastors and elders and deacons and youth workers and campus ministers are not only children of grace but also sinners greatly needing ongoing spiritual formation. Honest leaders look in the mirror and see all kinds of sins, such as pride, fear, envy, lust, anger, and laziness; they grapple with regret, insecurity, greed, doubt, and every other pressure and temptation the Enemy can throw at them.

Of course, this is no secret in our electronic age in which infamous moral failures are broadcast far and wide. Reports of sex scandals, embezzlement, plagiarism, or abuse are painfully familiar. But even so, tabloid headlines may actually conceal the mundane yet pervasive reality, namely, that every Christian leader labors under the weight of indwelling sin every day, all the way to heaven (in the office, at the dinner table, in traffic, at school, with the neighbors, with one's spouse, and so on).

Although all believers struggle with sin, the battle for Christian leaders is uniquely trying. The expectations placed upon them (e.g., to have answers, lead effectively, solve problems, expand the ministry, know God's will, and model holiness),[2] along with the isolation and loneliness that often come with the territory, can greatly intensify the ongoing spiritual battle: "Where do I go for help, with whom can I confide, . . . how much transparency is in order to help people relate to me and how much is unnecessary airing of dirty laundry, and—sinner that I am—how can I minimize the damage I do to my church?"[3]

---

2. Mark R. McMinn (*Why Sin Matters: The Surprising Relationship between Our Sin and God's Grace* [Wheaton: Tyndale, 2004], 50) contends that people typically expect perfection of their pastors.

3. M. Craig Barnes, *Yearning: Living between How It Is and How It Ought to Be* (Downers Grove, IL: InterVarsity Press, 1992), 149.

Further, if Peter Scazzero is correct—and I believe he is—that as the pastor goes, so goes the church,[4] then the importance of spiritual health and well-being for leaders can hardly be overstated. Care and support for those who lead thus become a priority for the body in general. We want to look at how godly leaders can advance in faith and holiness, and at the interplay of leader and people in this spiritual pursuit. Accordingly, this chapter addresses both leaders and those they lead on issues that matter to us all.

Marks of Maturing Leaders

J. I. Packer advises churches to choose pastors for their sanctity and devotion and not for skills and dynamism.[5] Some level of giftedness and practical capability is needed, of course, but the key traits of a pastor who's fit to lead God's people are spiritual. First Timothy 3 and Titus 1 similarly emphasize character-related qualifications for "overseers" or "elders,"[6] including the following:

- being "above reproach" and having a positive public reputation;
- moral uprightness (e.g., in regard to marriage and parenting);
- holding firmly to God's Word and being able to teach its truths;
- not being attached to earthly treasures;
- being able to manage and lead God's people;
- having patience, stability, and self-control; and
- not being conceited or young in the faith.

---

4. Peter Scazzero, *The Emotionally Healthy Church: A Strategy for Discipleship That Actually Changes Lives* (Grand Rapids: Zondervan, 2003), 36.
5. J. I. Packer, *Keep in Step with the Spirit* (Old Tappan, NJ: Revell, 1984), 98.
6. The terms for "elder," "overseer/bishop" and "pastor" are used more or less interchangeably in the New Testament (cf. Phil Newton, *Elders in Congregational Life* [Grand Rapids: Kregel, 2005], 33–36).

Maturing spiritual leaders must prioritize a commitment to and thorough knowledge of the Scriptures (2 Timothy 2:2, 15) so they can nourish believers with God's life-sustaining truth. Those who guide God's people may have strong relational skills, innovative ideas, and cultural or technological savvy, but if they're not strong in the Scriptures, the community suffers.

Moreover, maturing spiritual leaders usher God's people into his presence in fervent prayer (James 5:14). Other activities that draw leaders away from "prayer and the ministry of the word" (Acts 6:4 NIV) amount to distractions that should be delegated to other workers. A talented manager or motivator or socially dynamic "power personality" who's not setting the pace in pleading with the Lord, then, is simply unfit to lead in God's family.

What's more, these practices need to spring from leaders' personal lives. If spiritual acts are carried on just for the church's public consumption and are not grounded in personal devotion, one must conclude that the Lord and his Word are not cherished.[7] And so, those responsible for choosing leaders should have their ears tuned to hear if a candidate savors time in prayer and the Scriptures. And those aspiring to such positions should be on the lookout to see if a spiritual community is accustomed to rich prayer and diligent reflection on God's Word.

Christian leaders advancing in spiritual formation will seek God's strength to pursue peace in the body and yet not be held hostage to those who use tension or antagonism (i.e., "unpeace") to get leverage. This means addressing conflicts rather than avoiding them.[8] The pastor or ministry director who quickly complies with the contentious will

---

7. Charles Spurgeon, *Lectures to My Students* (Grand Rapids: Zondervan, 1979), 42, contends that the preacher "prays as an ordinary Christian, else he were a hypocrite."
8. Spurgeon (*Lectures to My Students*, 213) calls pastors to exercise "real courage . . . to go straight on at all hazards, though there should be none to give you a good word. I am astonished at the number of Christians who are afraid to speak the truth to their brethren."

become a magnet for opposition and lose the respect of the people, and this will spell trouble for the fellowship as a whole.

God's people also need leaders who humble themselves and demonstrate how to battle against sin. People "in the pew" have radar to pick up on preachers and other leaders who are too good to be true or act like they're above sin. The masquerade of "the pastor who has his act all together" does much harm. The apostle Paul exhibits a balance of humility and confidence: he's still far from perfect (Philippians 3:12), yet he puts himself forward as an example for others to follow on the maturation road (3:15, 17).

James Wilhoit gives a helpful description of Christian leaders who are effective in spiritual formation: "They are modeling brokenness, an openness to God and a humble modeling of Jesus."[9] The first step for a community to advance in spiritual formation has to do with the humble spiritual renewal of pastors and other leaders as individual followers of Christ. Such conduct by leaders creates a climate that's ripe for healthy spiritual formation among the people.

Mike Ensley asks some probing questions about why we're hesitant to accept the mortality of our leaders and of Christian "celebrities." Perhaps we desperately want to imagine that someday we'll get to the point where our besetting sins and nagging failures actually go away and that we'll finally be delivered and live fully above these struggles. Ensley's suspicion is that we project this intense longing onto our leaders and icons—they should exemplify spiritual victory and "be the ones that 'made it.' Then when they finally reveal to us that they are not, we condemn them, we cancel their legacies out, we pretend they were never the real thing."[10]

---

9. James C. Wilhoit, "Book Symposium: Response to Reviewers," *Journal of Spiritual Formation and Soul Care* 1.2 (2008): 247.

10. Mike Ensley, "Ray Boltz's Hunger for Community" (http://www.boundless. org/2005/articles/a0001918.cfm).

The solution to this dilemma has to be persistent teaching, learning, and following of the Bible so believers truly realize that, for spiritual leaders and everyone else, perfection is reserved for the life to come. Flawed Christian leaders may not communicate this biblical truth flawlessly, but often they can do so quite adequately. When people embrace this biblical realism while refusing to become complacent in the pursuit of holiness, godly leadership strikes a wise and healthy balance for the Christian community.

In light of this, for example, pulpit committees or church nominating teams should be careful not to recommend prospective leaders whose testimonies and references are success-slanted but who can't recognize their own sin battlefields and thus aren't ready to lead from a posture of humble reliance on God's grace. Those engaged in the process of appointing leaders need to be patient enough to dig deep and probe carefully in order to find a person who's truly wrestled with the Lord and faced down his or her own twisted heart and propensity to self-exaltation—someone who's got a healthy suspicion of self and seeks accountability alongside other maturing Christian leaders.

In the case of the pastoral search process, believers need to have eyes wide open: *we're sinners, and we're hiring a sinner to lead us.* Such frankness during the search process helps churches and candidates gain necessary information about each other's ways of dealing with temptation and personal failure. Keeping "hush-hush" about such things, by contrast, reinforces a "don't ask, don't tell" culture that doesn't face up to important spiritual realities, thus failing to grow through various sin struggles. If candidates and committees know themselves well (Jeremiah 17:9) and are willing to speak candidly to each other, an atmosphere of grace and humble support can be created within which to battle sin and pursue holiness together.

Exercising Spiritual Leadership

Let's probe further into the *exercise* of spiritual leadership within the church or a Christian group or organization. For example, how should pastors go about the work of shepherding God's flock so as to take full account of their own sinful condition and the imperfection of their perspectives on the life of the church? And how should a church or Christian group fashion its authority structure so as to protect the body from unnecessary risks and temptations, providing all with healthy boundaries and safeguards? There's a balance in maintaining vigilance about sin's danger without creating an atmosphere of paranoia.[11] Here are some key measures:

Praying for Spiritual Leaders

Churches and Christian groups should expect Satan strategically to target their pastors and leaders with a particular intensity; not expecting such opposition is being naive. Leaders have a special need for "prayer cover." In connection with putting on the armor of God for spiritual warfare, Paul charges the Ephesians to lift him up in prayer: "To that end keep alert with all perseverance, making supplication for all the saints, and also for me, that words may be given to me in opening my mouth boldly to proclaim the mystery of the gospel, for which I am an ambassador in chains, that I may declare it boldly, as I ought to speak" (6:18–20). Ministry leaders face exceptional pressures and are held to special standards (2 Corinthians 11:28; James 3:1), and in this high calling they greatly need God's protection and spiritual support.

---

11. It's appropriate to require criminal background checks of all vocational and lay leaders, including all who work with children or teens. Further, it's wise to be stringent and cautious about allowing people into leadership roles; they should be well known and proven in terms of character and gifts before being considered to be pastors, elders, deacons, and the like.

I've asked the people of my church especially to pray for me on Saturdays. Typically as I'm making final preparations for Sunday worship and especially to deliver the Word of God, the Enemy comes at me with all kinds of temptations and deceptions to distract and drag me down. "Please pray that I would be quick to run to Christ in these times and that the Lord would not only sustain me but also fill me with hope in his life-changing grace and with zeal for the spreading of his reign! By the way, the Lord has a track record of doing this—Sundays that follow those, shall we say, bleak Saturdays routinely turn out to be bright with hope and joy in Christ."

Admission of Sin by Leaders

In addition, pastors and leadership teams must see to it that a message of honesty about sin is proclaimed and modeled—and that it permeates the life of the church. Humble acceptance of the "still growing" state of all believers, leaders included, is crucial for shaping a culture of honest Christian community. And that's best achieved not when others point fingers but when pastors, elders, and lay leaders themselves openly admit their need of God's renewing grace and ask people to pray for their progress in Christlikeness. When such transparency is in place within a fellowship, leaders can go further and speak of their accountability relationships, support groups, and other measures they take to battle sin.

This combination of humility and zeal for holiness is catching—members of the community can relate to the leader because a realistic and honest picture has been painted. And on that basis, they can join in with their pastor's or teacher's contagious quest for the joy of holiness. By contrast, when leaders come off as "saintly" or are put up on a pedestal, people may be impressed, but they'll have a hard time identifying with such heroes and difficulty gaining hope and inspiration from them.

A word is in order about just *how* open Christian leaders should be about their sin struggles and the unique pressures and burdens they endure. How much openness is "enough"? When does public confession actually become counterproductive and end up undermining a leader's position? On the one hand, "confess your sins to one another" and "admonish one another" are for the whole church. "Forgive one another" isn't just for laypeople. Peter is assigned a key role as, shall we say, the "lead pastor" of the newly founded church in Jerusalem, but he had a track record of failings and a tendency to cower in fear rather than act in faith (Galatians 2:11–14). Paul is presented in the New Testament as a pioneering missionary pastor who leads the church outward into the Roman world, announcing the good news, but he's certainly not perfect. The tiff between Paul and Barnabas is a vivid example of imperfect leaders in action (Acts 15:36–41).

On the other hand, imperfection in the lives of leaders doesn't disqualify or sideline them from their ministry calling.[12] Peter and Paul carry on with mission work and pastoral duties, their own deficiencies notwithstanding. Timid Timothy isn't urged to retreat from leadership for his faltering faith, but rather to step forward depending on God's grace and power even when he feels woefully inadequate (2 Timothy 2:7–8, 12, 16). In short, the New Testament doesn't see indwelling

---

12. Of course, there are sin calamities that do, in fact, disqualify Christian leaders from carrying on in their office. Flagrant acts and patterns of sin by those who have positions of spiritual leadership reveal a lack of fitness to lead. To be sure, it can be difficult to discern just what kind of sin fits this description; where is the line, e.g., between sin that can be confessed and put behind a pastor and sin that must be confessed and for which one must step down from the pastorate? Kent Hughes and John Armstrong argue that adultery disqualifies one from pastoral leadership for life ("Why Adulterous Pastors Should Not Be Restored" *Christianity Today* [Apr. 3, 1995]: 33–38), while Kenneth Kantzer ("The Road to Restoration: How Should the Church Treat Its Fallen Leaders?" *Christianity Today* [Nov. 20, 1987]: 19–23) is open, though cautiously, to the restoration to leadership of pastors who've experienced moral failure. David Neff notes how 1 Cor. 6:18 singles out physical sexual sin as being uniquely devastating—it destroys trust, it thus denies one's legitimacy as a leader, and it ruins a leader's image ("Are All Sins Created Equal?" *Christianity Today* [Nov. 20, 1987]: 20–21).

sin as justifying withdrawal from ministry, nor does it portray church leaders as wallowing in their failings or as dwelling on them to such an extent that people lose hope for growth in Christ. A balance is in order: facing the facts, humbly confessing, asking for prayerful support, and then looking ahead—leaders and people—with trust in the forgiving, empowering grace of God!

Accountability Relationships

Another key measure for fighting sin as a leader is to commit to accountability relationships with other believers (and for vocational pastors, ideally with other leaders from outside one's own congregation). Such partnerships help leaders gain ground in the fight against sin by challenging each other on a regular basis. Commonly within such groups there are pointed questions to be asked of all members, for example regarding one's devotional life (including experience in the Word and prayer), key relationships (including marital faithfulness and God-honoring friendships), thought life and viewing habits, use of time, financial practices, and more. Committing to accountability is a way leaders can say before the Lord and his people that they need and invite the support of others.

Though the aim of accountability groups may be good, Jonathan Dodson points out that in practice they often degenerate into legalism or license.[13] Either we perform to impress one another or avoid predetermined punishments (legalism), or we treat group sharing like a confessional booth, handing out cheap grace and cheap peace (license). These errors are remedied by placing the gospel at the center; accountability fellowships need to orbit around Jesus and not rules.

I appreciate Dodson's cautions. In every kind of interaction among believers we must steer the ship between legalism and license—or, one could say, between despair over indwelling sin and euphoria about

---

13. Jonathan Dodson, *Fight Clubs: Gospel-Centered Discipleship* (Austin, TX: Austin City Life eBook, 2009, http://www.austincitylife.org/fightclubs.htm), 19–22.

gains in godliness.[14] In the end, however, it would be unwise to throw out the baby of accountability with the bathwater of legalism or license.

Living within Limits

Christian leaders with limitless responsibility are on an express train to burnout or, worse, to be ministry dropouts. Eugene Peterson's helpful essay "The Unbusy Pastor" boils shepherding down to three things: praying, preaching, and listening. Busyness is a sign not of commitment but of betrayal. He contends that pastors get busy for one of two reasons: vanity or laziness (laziness makes one busy through failing to take charge of the appointment calendar so as to preserve times for study, rest, and refreshment). "How can I lead people into the quiet place beside still waters if I am in perpetual motion?"[15]

God calls Christian leaders to be in conversation with him, to be drenched in and then expound his Word, and to listen compassionately, in unhurried leisure, to the fears and hopes of his people. That's it—the pastor who prays, preaches, and listens is fulfilling God's call. Others may summarize the minister's duties a bit differently (I'd add that most pastors simply must do some amount of administrative work). But one way or the other, definite limits have to be set, and then pastor and people need to agree together to respect those boundaries as a way to move the church forward under God's blessing.

---

14. Or, for that matter, between the alternatives in other false polarizations that crop up in the church, such as hope for healing or expectation of suffering; divine sovereignty or human responsibility; God as transcendent or immanent; ministry of word or deed—the list could go on.

15. Eugene Peterson, "The Unbusy Pastor," in *The Contemplative Pastor* (Grand Rapids: Eerdmans, 1989), 19. Peter Scazzero (*Emotionally Healthy Spirituality* [Nashville: Integrity, 2006], 34–35) identifies "living without limits" as one of the top ten symptoms of emotionally unhealthy spirituality. Despite the idea that Christians are always to give and help and serve others, being human means having limitations—we're not God. Self-care is not a selfish act, but simply good stewardship of one's life. And it's necessary if we are to give meaningful care to others.

Plurality of Leaders

Another measure to help safeguard leaders and leadership is plurality, that is, leading together and not in isolation. New Testament passages about elders speak in terms of multiple elders for the local church (Acts 14:23; Titus 1:5).[16] This need not be understood as a leveling of all pastoral responsibilities; there's still room for a senior member of the team or one who's "first among equals" (perhaps a paid teaching elder would have this distinctive role within a team made up mostly of lay elders). The key is to make sure the vital work of prayerfully leading the church, or directing a Christian ministry, is not entirely handed over to an individual.

Consider the wisdom of Proverbs: "Where there is no guidance, a people falls, but in an abundance of counselors there is safety" (Proverbs 11:14). "For by wise guidance you can wage your war, and in abundance of counselors there is victory" (Proverbs 24:6). Assigning the tasks of teaching and guiding God's people to a team of spiritually qualified leaders, frankly, is a crucial step for fighting sin and growing in holiness. By contrast, when a pastor resists the partnership of duly appointed elders who can assist and support in the good work and who can help encourage and caution him as a pastor, it signals misguided thinking and risky isolation that endanger both leader and people. Believers should be on the lookout for the red flag of isolated leaders before joining a given Christian fellowship.

Counsel and Enrichment for Leaders

Since all Christian leaders are vulnerable to sin and weakness, there are times when they need special support. What's more, as mentioned above, church leaders face exceptional trials and uniquely intense

---

16. Phil Newton, *Elders in Congregational Life* (Kregel: Grand Rapids, 205), 37–40.

spiritual pressures, and so, along with temptation, it's not uncommon to run into exhaustion or depletion of one kind or another.

While many counseling needs can be met through the mutual ministries of the body offering a listening ear, loving support, and biblical admonition, there are times when a specially trained helper (i.e., a skilled counselor) is needed to come alongside a Christian leader over a sustained period of time. Humble and honest pastors will accept the fact that, in their humanity, they may well need this kind of help at times. The focus of attention in the counseling office might be issues of personal emotional well-being or an understanding of one's temperament and personality. Or there may be a need for marriage counseling or family therapy.

Years ago I heard a respected evangelical pastor describe how he and his wife were receiving marriage counseling. I was startled at first. But it was healthy—he was open about their struggles and the value of a counselor's help, and this demonstrated a humble willingness to learn and grow. Our family was going through some rough growing pains a few years ago, so we sat down with a Christian counselor who helped us recognize a few of our unwritten relational "rules" and work toward new patterns for life at home. I've had the privilege of meeting one-on-one with a therapist to help me process some confusing life transitions and to get a better understanding of how my mind and emotions function. Those sessions were a gift from the Lord.

For some there may be a stigma around the idea of counseling—it's for the weak, it's disgraceful, or it's just a bunch of "psychobabble." But earnest believers who want to gain ground against sin will not fall for such caricatures. A thoughtful "outsider" can be especially well positioned to see and hear things in us we don't notice, and these can be keys for moving past one impasse or another toward greater spiritual maturity.

Not only must leaders themselves take to heart the value of counseling, but churches and ministry organizations in general also need to give this consideration. For instance, when forming a ministry leader's benefits package, it's fitting to build in resources to assist with occasional counseling needs. Some years ago our family was able to draw on our denominational district office's Minister's Assistance Program, which covered 90 percent of the cost of up to ten counseling sessions per year. On a tight budget, this kind of help was the difference between receiving counseling and simply having to go without it.

Following the Leader

A church or Christian organization with a corporate inclination to resist its leaders' initiatives is a social system that's at odds with Scripture: "We ask you, brothers, to respect those who labor among you and are over you in the Lord and admonish you, and to esteem them very highly in love because of their work. Be at peace among yourselves" (1 Thessalonians 5:12–13). To contend against pastors and elders and seek to wrest the leadership of God's people from their hands is to fail to express respect and esteem, and it is to work against peace in the body.

No doubt some believers will be keenly aware of their pastors' flaws, and they may respond with reticence or even by defying the guidance and oversight of those leaders. Those who've been burned by authority figures who abused their power may have difficulty supporting other leaders. Further, in some cases it may be that members of a fellowship have superior gifts to those in leadership, or through experience or learning they may conclude that the directives of their pastors and elders should not be embraced. It's possible for cases to arise in which nonleaders do indeed recognize a serious deficiency, and when that happens, a leadership team that's spiritually sensitive will take constructive criticism to heart.

Moreover, there's definitely a place within the scheme of decision making for "the voice of the people." In the early church, after the Twelve had taken the lead in uncovering a problem and urging the people to identify several workers to serve tables, we read, "And what they said pleased the whole gathering" (Acts 6:5). It mattered that there was "popular" support for this step. And in Acts 15:22, after the apostles and elders had spoken pointedly to the question of whether or not one had to be circumcised in order to be saved, and after James asserted that the answer was no, we read, "Then it seemed good to the apostles and the elders, with the whole church, to choose men from among them and send them to Antioch with Paul and Barnabas." Here again, the plan for communicating and implementing this action involved "the whole church"—the people in general.

And yet, in our democratically minded day and age, and with our post-Watergate suspicion of authority, the greater risk in the North American church setting is to neutralize the authorization of designated leaders to lead. We're prone to take the idea of "checks and balances" to a high level, even to extremes, with the result that leaders may end up with responsibility but no authority to lead, and instead they're expected somehow to implement the will of the masses.

Against that backdrop God's people need to hear Hebrews 13:17 afresh: "Obey your leaders and submit to them, for they are keeping watch over your souls, as those who will have to give an account. Let them do this with joy and not with groaning, for that would be of no advantage to you." The clarifications offered already imply that this is not a mindless or unquestioning obedience, but rather an intelligent affirmation of God-appointed leaders.[17] It's urgent for believers to reflect on how their conduct brings either joy or groaning to their

---

17. That the "leaders" in view are spiritual authorities (and not, e.g., merely village elders or city rulers) is directly implied by Hebrews 13:7 in which the "leaders" (same Greek term) are those who had spoken the Word of God to the people.

leaders—and to see that a joy-giving affirmation of them is good for the whole body. Making leaders groan is "of no advantage to you."

Why are believers charged with obeying their spiritual leaders? It's *because* those pastors and elders keep watch over the souls of the members of the body. By God's help, and with the prayerful support of his people, church leaders are seeking to build up his people in faith by the way they lead; they're looking to see the Lord infuse joy and hope into people's hearts. That's their aim for which they must "give an account" before the Lord. Even though imperfect leaders don't achieve this goal perfectly, surely it is worthy of the people's affirmation.

Chapter 10

THE MICROSCOPE
OF MARRIAGE

Convincing people not to drink the water in places where it isn't carefully purified is difficult because the microorganisms that lurk in it aren't visible to the naked eye. So too, persuading children (and the rest of us) to wash hands frequently is hard to do because the germs we pick up from railings and doorknobs and all kinds of objects are invisible; hands may look clean and still be very dirty. But if you enlist the services of a microscope and make the unseen dangers visible, the need to take precautions becomes obvious.

The closeness God intends married couples to experience has the side effect of putting sin under a microscope. As a result, a relationship rich with sweetness can be soured through disappointment and dismay. Therefore, it's tremendously important for believers to look closely at the role of indwelling sin within marriage. By doing so, husbands and wives may steer clear of unreasonable expectations and pave the way for unions of grace and peace. Further, churches that anticipate how sin often rears its ugly head within marriages can give couples strategies to limit its damage and build healthy foundations instead. What's more, many of the pressures of marriage are similar to those faced in any close friendship, and so the present chapter can speak to singles as well, as they grapple with sin and nurture deep, lasting relationships.

I turn to the topic of marriage cautiously—mostly because I feel I still have so much to learn. In my single, young adult years I was wildly idealistic and overconfident about married life. My marriage, I determined, would be a stellar example of selfless service and overflowing joy. I made up my mind to communicate with my future wife in perpetual kindness and affirmation and transparency, thus preventing any tension or misunderstanding from cropping up between us. I believed that God was with me (that was true) and that he wanted the best for me (true again), so I felt it would only be right to chart a course of radical godliness and love, thus forming an exemplary, countercultural marriage (this is where my thinking was desperately simplistic).

One day, when I was a student at a Christian college, my idealism erupted in response to a psychology professor's lecture on the issue of divorce. The gist of his comments was to say that God hates divorce (Malachi 2:16) and that it's always a sorrowful thing, that the better solution is reconciliation, but that sometimes divorce happens—even in Christian marriages. I objected: it sounded like the prof was making excuses for divorce, letting the camel's nose into the tent and thus opening the way for untold misery. And it seemed to me that the clear teaching of the Bible about the permanence of marriage ("What therefore God has joined together, let not man separate") was being marginalized and that sinful encroachments from the world were being condoned. My professor was taken aback, having not imagined his message would be heard in such a way. He commended my enthusiasm for lifelong marriage and reassured the class that his presentation was not to be understood as condoning sin or lowering biblical standards.

But, in fact, I had overreacted in my zeal—a zeal resting on inadequate knowledge of the fuller biblical teaching about indwelling sin. I hadn't yet truly grappled with the pervasive presence of sin in believers and with the slowness and intricate complexity of God's sanctifying work. Any toleration of sin's ravages I saw as compromising and rationalizing. Only over many years of studying the Scriptures and learning through experience have I developed a more nuanced and (I believe) more adequate set of expectations about how life unfolds for genuine Christians.

I turn attention to the topic of marriage with a keen consciousness of my need to grow in understanding and empathy and wisdom. Cheryl and our children would confirm that God is far from finished with the overhaul project he's doing in my life. Nevertheless, I want to share some insights about marriage so as to keep both biblical realism and biblical hope in view.

Wedded Bliss and Other Marriage Expectations

In every society history has known, in all cultures, in every land and across all time, it has been universally true that those who've married have said "I do" to sinners. Every bride and groom has brought to marriage a heart in which rebellion against the Lord God is ongoing. In no wedding throughout the history of the human race have husband and wife been joined to form a union free from the stains of sin.

This claim, of course, is simply an extension of the fact that all people are sinners. Further, despite the joy and hope believing couples bring with them to the altar, even the most devout followers of Christ enter into unions tarnished by the spiritual inclinations and failings they carry into the relationship. Moreover, as Larry Crabb notes, every marriage between honest, self-examining people at some time reaches a "seemingly irredeemable low point" due to sin's destructive influence.[1]

That sobering fact needs to be taken into account when shaping marriage expectations.[2] I don't mean to rain on anyone's wedding parade or paint a grim picture. Maybe you're envisioning my officiating at a wedding, standing before the beaming couple and warning them, "Dearly beloved, it's all downhill from here!" So let me try to put things in perspective. There is, in fact, a great deal of "wedded bliss" to enjoy within a Christian marriage.

I speak from experience. Despite our faults, Cheryl and I have found a great deal of joy and spiritual support walking with Christ together. We're in our twenty-fifth year of marriage now, and the three children God has given us are in their teens and early twenties. We've shared countless smiles and times of loving support; I couldn't number the occasions when just coming home to be with my wife has been exactly what I needed. Innumerable times we've built each other up, learned from one another, and comforted each other amid hardships. God's gift of marriage to Cheryl has been a rich blessing to me, and I don't want in any way to minimize this beautiful truth.

Nevertheless, expectations surrounding marriage are sometimes simply out of touch with reality. And I don't just mean the expectations of naive young people longing to wed their sweethearts, but also the anticipations and imaginations of many husbands and wives year after year, decade after decade, in the thick of married life. We bring some lofty hopes to the altar and cling to them over time. And yet, a careful look at such expectations reveals that they're often lopsided—that is, they typically place heavier demands on one's spouse than oneself.

Sabrina Beasley addresses this unevenness: "Somehow we have been convinced that our spouses should be like fairytale royalty—always

---

1. Larry Crabb, *Marriage Builder* (Grand Rapids: Zondervan, 1992), 109.
2. Regarding marriage expectations, note Paul Tripp's recent work, *What Did You Expect?: Redeeming the Realities of Marriage* (Wheaton: Crossway, 2010).

perfect, always attractive, always sensitive to our needs. Yet we don't expect to be treated with the same standard. We expect our spouses to be tolerant of our sins, but not the other way around."[3] So there's a double standard that crops up when it comes to marriage expectations: a man's hope for the maturity, kindness, patience, beauty, and overall "wonderfulness" of his wife knows no bounds, but at the same time he's more ready and willing to let himself off the hook when his bad habits and ungodly side come out. Similar things could be said about how wives have higher expectations for their husbands than for themselves. That we're keenly aware of others' sins but not so willing to acknowledge our own is not a problem unique to the marriage relationship, but rather a struggle endemic to the human condition. But when you mix the lofty dreams of wedded bliss with this double-standard tendency, it can create a dangerous brew.

And, ironically, this may be especially problematic in Christian marriages. After all, the Bible paints stunningly lofty visions of the marriage union. The Song of Solomon provides an extended discourse on the rapture of sexual love in marriage, fanning the flames of anticipation. And the teaching on marriage in Ephesians 5, in which husbands are taught to love their wives as Christ loved the church, raises the bar of self-giving love to the highest level: what greater expression of true devotion is there than Christ's death for his sinful enemies?

Thoughtful Christians who meditate on these visions of marriage are bound to have their hopes raised high and, in light of such yearnings, may be tempted to conceal their own foibles and flaws before the wedding (or even after it) to sustain the Grand Dream. If spouses fear they can be accepted and loved only if they match the biblical ideal, they'll fall tragically into a performance-based relationship mindset and, very possibly, a performance-driven response to God.

---

3. Sabrina Beasley, "Help! I Married a Sinner," www.familylife.com. The story of how her fiancé concealed his obsession with football during the engagement period is told with humor and humble honesty.

Or if believers read the Bible selectively and dwell on glorious visions of marital union but fail to come to terms with the broader biblical message about indwelling sin, a dreamy notion of marital bliss may be formed—and then dashed in short order by real life together as sinners. The Puritans provide an instructive example. They knew their Bibles and realized that marriage was for sinners; it was understood that to marry was to be joined to a sinner, a child of Adam. In light of this, one was certainly not to expect perfection.[4]

Gospel-Centered Marriage

The solution for our interpersonal troubles is found, first of all, in knowing and trusting Jesus Christ. Horizontal relationships are never brought into the right, redemptive light until those involved have their vertical relations with God put in order. This is not to imply that non-Christians cannot have good marriages. The point, rather, is that their good marriages will be limited by the absence of both love for Jesus Christ and a corresponding love for others that flow from heartfelt thanks for his undeserved kindness.

One might argue that the lack of such religious experience is not necessarily a flaw in a marriage, but from the Scriptures we must conclude otherwise. Marriage has been designed by God and given to humans as a blessing from his hand to be received with gratitude. What's more, marriage is an earthly parable of heavenly realities—a temporal visual aid to show us and all the world what a glorious love relationship exists (and will exist forever) between Jesus Christ and his bride, the church. This "vertical" aspect is the very heart of marriage, and it must be rightly perceived and embraced as priority one. Only those who know and trust in Christ can fully appreciate this symbolism.

---

4. Leland Ryken, *Worldly Saints: The Puritans as They Really Were* (Grand Rapids: Zondervan, 1986), 51; cf. John Piper, *This Momentary Marriage* (Wheaton: Crossway, 2009), 48.

And yet, for the Christian couple, marriage enrichment is always needed—even between godly spouses who've patiently learned to care for each other (perhaps over many decades) and who revel in the sweet love of Christ together. Spiritual formation is a journey more than a destination. What's more, advances of godliness require ongoing reinforcement, or they'll fade and the relationship will slip backward. A growing Christian marriage is like keeping house: if you don't dust and clean on a regular basis, things get messy.[5] There's no coasting in marriage; when husbands and wives take each other for granted and assume all is well, closeness declines and the Devil gets a foothold.

The best platform on which to grow a God-honoring Christian marriage is the gospel; we need gospel-centered marriages in order to exalt the Lord and bring maximum blessing to one another and those around us. In a gospel-centered marriage, husbands and wives are conscious, first of all, of how much they've been forgiven by Christ. Although undeserving of such kindness, Christian husbands and wives have been freely justified, fully reconciled to the Lord, and adopted as his beloved children forever.

A Christ-centered, gospel-shaped marriage relationship is animated by a reflex that "looks up"—that is, by an inclination over and over to look away to Jesus and stand in awe of his amazing grace. We consider what wrath we deserved and how we were dead and lost in sin apart from Christ, and we're moved to praise the One who saved us. A gospel-centered marriage is not just one in which we give thanks for God's love, but a relationship fueled by and aimed at heartfelt praise!

In *This Momentary Marriage*, John Piper calls believing spouses to focus on Christ's forgiving and bearing with them and then to let this grateful spirit become the basis for forgiving and forbearing their

---

5. Dave Harvey, *When Sinners Say "I Do"* (Wapwallopen, PA: Shepherd Press, 2007), 29, 138–40. Dealing with sin is the key to a thriving marriage.

spouses.[6] The gospel thus becomes the footing for mercy in marriage. Larry Crabb makes the further observation that if you ask your spouse to meet your basic security and significance needs as a person, he or she is being asked to do what only God can do.[7] The vertical relationship must be established first, and then upon that bedrock of secure love one is free to give and receive marital love in healthy ways. Dave Harvey drives home a related point: it's through the gospel that we gain power to resist sin[8]—that is, by receiving and savoring the loving grace of God in one's own life, a person is energized to fight sin and extend true love to others—including to one's spouse.

Imperfect and unfinished sinners that we are, we tend to lose sight of the gospel and the glorious grace of God, so it's important in marriage to find ways to help each other keep looking to Christ and continue taking joy in God's saving love. To do this, we need all the encouragement we can get. Time spent together in the Word of God and in prayer, not to mention unhurried conversation about each other's spiritual lives, is an investment of immense value. Failing to come together in spiritual practices, by contrast, shapes a marriage in which God becomes either compartmentalized in isolated facets of a person's life, or (worse yet) increasingly remote and seemingly irrelevant.

The "one another" commands addressed above (see chapter 8) find a practical application within marriage relationships: encourage one another to keep trusting the Lord—that is, to fix your eyes on Jesus and be transformed through beholding the glory of the Lord (2 Corinthians 3:18). Forgive one another, bear with one another as husband and wife (I know that's not very flattering), and confess your sins to one another—be open and honest. (After all, your spouse probably knows your sins better than you do, so why not speak truthfully?)

---

6. John Piper, *This Momentary Marriage*, 55; cf. Col. 3:13.
7. Larry Crabb, *Marriage Builder*, 21–22.
8. Dave Harvey, *When Sinners Say "I Do,"* 25.

A commitment to reciprocal love reminds us that not only do I need to extend kindness to my beloved, but I need to receive it as well. "One another" is inherently a two-way street, and in order to obey such biblical injunctions, believing spouses must face up to the implication of their own sin and need of horizontal mercy. To put it differently, the Golden Rule is Jesus' way of teaching his followers to give each other the love and kindness they'd want to receive (Matthew 7:12). Reciprocity is a fundamental guideline for discipleship, including that special path of maturation God gives to believing spouses who challenge and support each other.

John Piper offers an extended analogy that can help Christian couples limit the odor of sin within their relationships: Your marriage is like a grassy field, pleasant and beautiful. But with time you and your spouse stumble upon cow pies in the pasture—in fact, in some seasons of marriage, the cow pies seem to be everywhere. Through a mutual commitment of forbearance and forgiveness, however, a husband and wife create a compost pile onto which they shovel those cow pies. Honesty admits that there are a lot of stinky cow pies in the field. But there are many beautiful flowers and trees and rolling hills as well. One thing is sure: "We will not pitch our tent by the compost pile. We will only go there when we must. This is a gift of grace that we will give each other again and again and again—because we are chosen and holy and loved."[9] The idea is not to baptize sin or blithely admit that there's a big mess in our marriage and leave it at that. "Cow pie behaviors" are to be fought vigorously, and holiness is to be pursued with hope. The point is simply that we must expect sin to crop up and need our attention, so make a plan to clean up the mess and carry on looking to Jesus.

---

9. John Piper, *This Momentary Marriage*, 59. The analogy is not offered as a concession to sin but to avoid being naive about the sheer reality of lingering imperfection in our marriages (60).

A grace-based marriage is one in which it's safe to admit fault, safe to confess sins—after all, you're confessing to one who also has many failings, and you're confessing to someone who's basking in the prior grace of Christ and should thus be ready to relay that grace to you. The gospel of Jesus Christ is not just about coming to Christ in the first place. It's a work of God to exalt his glory through our salvation *and* ongoing sanctification—and our experience of this continuing grace is profoundly refreshing and motivating. In marriage it motivates husbands and wives to create a "safe zone" for failure, freedom to stumble and fall. Craig Barnes helpfully puts it this way: in marriage we don't manage our needs, we confess them. "We don't mend each other's brokenness; we just hold it tightly."[10]

Beasley notes, however, that "unfortunately, couples are often so preoccupied by taking score of each other's shortcomings that they miss out on one of the greatest blessings of marriage—the benefit of not having to live under pressure to be perfect. It's the one relationship, other than our relationship with Christ, where we can feel secure knowing that someone loves us for who we are, warts and all, and there is great peace in that."[11] There's freedom in Christian marriage, freedom to be honest, to struggle for holiness together, to falter and flop on the ground and weep together. And freedom to look up again into the face of Jesus and remind each other of his enduring love.

This kind of freedom to fail could be taken as a license to sin—if you're loved and accepted no matter what, you're at liberty to do as you wish, right? And our wishes can be quite ungodly. But let's consider how Scripture speaks to this matter. After long discourses on the beauty of the gospel and justification by faith and not works in Romans 3–5, Paul anticipates that people will wonder if grace gives license to sin: "What shall we say then? Are we to continue in sin that grace may abound? By no means! How can we who died to sin still live in it?" (Romans 6:1–2). There's freedom in Christ, and it includes the

---

10. M. Craig Barnes, *Yearning*, 93.
11. Sabrina Beasley, "Help! I Married a Sinner."

freedom of knowing one is loved despite ongoing flaws and struggles and sin battles. But the God-intended design of grace is that it would inspire not license and rebellion but grateful thanks and a deeper zeal to honor the Lord.

This same dynamic is present in gospel-centered, grace-based marriages. The safety and security of marital love and the freedom to fail as an imperfect husband or wife—knowing you are still accepted, knowing you're not condemned—reflect God's unchanging love and inspire both horizontal affection and vertical praise. In other words, it has just the opposite effect of that which is feared—grace inspires obedience to God, not sin against him. And grace from your spouse inspires a renewed appreciation that you're loved and a refreshed desire to bless your beloved.

A marriage that's "safe" in this way allows spouses to drop their guard. Further, it works against the blaming reflex and helps a believer look in the mirror first. Dave Harvey contends that when you see yourself as a sinner, your spouse is no longer the biggest problem in the marriage—you are.[12] And from that humble position, a growing disciple of Christ is motivated to grant grace to his or her spouse. Paul Tripp advises struggling couples to let go of blaming with this counsel: "No matter how much you are aware of the failure of the other person, you have to embrace the fact that you're biggest marital problem is still you."[13]

Blaming is a dead end—it leads nowhere. But when Christian husbands and wives share a gospel-centered vision for marriage and thus reject the impulse to condemn their faltering partners, their Christlike conduct defuses the need to blame and creates freedom— for example, the freedom to confess your sin to your spouse, knowing that the confession will be received by a fellow sinner who also savors grace and also cherishes your support.

---

12. Dave Harvey, *When Sinners Say "I Do,"* 41, 52, 67.
13. Rebecca Grace, "Messy Marriages in the Hands of a Gracious God: Interview with Paul David Tripp," *AFA Journal* (Feb. 2009), www.onenewsnow.com.

Paul Tripp wisely warns, "We can't rest and relax, because marriage is war, and I don't mean war with the other person. It's spiritual war." Satan has wreaked havoc in Christian marriages, and much of that damage comes from not understanding how to respond to indwelling sin and from a lack of gospel-centered lives. In the journey of faith and the battle against sin, we need each other—and believing husbands and wives depend on one another's spiritual support more than any one else's. Tripp goes on: "I'm more and more persuaded as I study Scripture that my life is intended by God to be a community project." It's through community, marriage, and family that we actually become more of what God has designed us to be.[14] In other words, God uses sinners to pursue and rebuke and encourage other sinners—as Nathan did for David (2 Samuel 12:1–14), and as husbands and wives in Christ can do for one another.[15]

Lofty hopes and unrealistic dreams of sheer bliss in marriage have set many couples up for disappointment. Christian marriages, ironically, may be strengthened by the *lowering* of certain expectations spouses place upon each other. Infusing a marriage with the freedom to fail and the security of Christlike love actually inspires marital affection and a zeal for greater closeness and commitment to one another. Of course, there remains a need for wisdom to discern, as a loving husband or wife, when and how strongly to urge your spouse to stride forward in the obedience of faith and when to calmly, kindly wait—to forbear, to accept the existence of weaknesses or sin struggles in the life of your beloved even while prayerfully seeking God's sanctifying touch in his or her life. Surely the moment of such decision making is a great time also to look in the mirror and consider how *you* need to forsake sin that you bring into the relationship.

I've had many opportunities to sit down with engaged couples to work through a premarital counseling process and with married

14. Ibid.
15. Dave Harvey, *When Sinners Say "I Do,"* 116.

couples whose relationships have been in distress. I was surprised at first to find some engaged couples already struggling with relationship dynamics that resemble those from troubled marriages: she doesn't trust his family; he doesn't respect her handling of money; they can't agree on a parenting strategy or a budget or something else. In divorce courts the claim of "irreconcilable differences" is often made; the two people just aren't compatible. But the truth is, apart from God's grace to and through us, all marriages are damaged by incompatibility in one serious degree or another.

A couple I met with was in what I'd call a relationship emergency: there were angry words, finger-pointing; all kindness had vanished from their marriage. Both of them would have said they considered themselves to be Christians, and yet there was no breaking through to the place where relational healing could happen—no getting beyond blaming and accusing each other of one fault after another. A devious tactic of the Enemy is to prompt flawed spouses to pass blame as long as they believe the other party is *more* at fault. The perception of a greater guilt borne by the other person thus interferes with accepting responsibility for one's own failings and obstructs the flow of grace within the marriage relationship.

But when someone dares to admit his own sin failings without demanding a reciprocal confession from his spouse—when one person is willing simply to say, "I've hurt you and I apologize; please forgive me"—a ray of grace breaks through the dark clouds, animosity is defused, and hope begins to return. This is the gospel in motion, being worked out in hard ways that nonetheless can breathe life into dying relationships—*forgive each other as the Lord has forgiven you* (Colossians 3:13). We don't erase all sin from our hearts here and now, but the Lord is ready to help his people build grace-based marriages that endure, and even flourish, because they're saturated in his forgiving love. Grace happens—God is at work in broken lives today. And there's always hope when spouses humbly turn to Christ together.

Chapter 11

SIN, SANCTIFICATION, AND DIVINE SOVEREIGNTY

When indwelling sin, progressive sanctification, and the sovereignty of God are put "on the table" together, questions arise: How can divine sovereignty and ongoing sin coexist? What kind of supreme authority is it that tolerates perpetual mutiny? Is the reach of God's ruling "arm" limited, thus accounting for the pockets of defiance that persist in believers' hearts? Is genuine sovereignty even a possibility when sin still festers?

If it is, how does it account for the pervasive and harrowing effects of sin? Can the notion of God's supremacy be so elastic that it encompasses motives and actions that contradict his reign? Why would a sovereign God allow history to unfold in such a way that sin endures, like a clinging parasite, in the hearts of his people? To put it differently, why does God act within the grand scheme of redemptive history, from creation to fall to redemption and on to the final consummation, so that his people are transformed gradually and not immediately? If sanctification is supposed to be progressive and not instantaneous, that makes indwelling sin a necessary part of the plan. So does God approve of sin's ongoing presence in believers' lives?

The problem of reconciling divine sovereignty with remaining sin is exacerbated by two factors. First, progressive sanctification isn't always progressive; sometimes it stalls or even reverses as faltering believers stray from the path.[1] The witness of numerous believers whose lives are portrayed in the Scriptures (not to mention our own lives) is that growth often takes place by "three steps forward and two steps back." So why should maturation involves such fits and starts? Second, progressive sanctification runs into the massive obstacle of "besetting sins"—ruts along the discipleship road where believers repeatedly get stuck, particular temptations that seem insurmountable. How can a sovereign God tolerate such persistent defiance? What could he be up to in this messy scheme?

Our God Does Whatever He Pleases

To put things in perspective, let's step back and briefly note some bedrock biblical facts about God—who God is and what he's like. Isaiah 40 provides a panoramic view: God is great *and* good; he's majestic and merciful. The Lord is Maker of all things and answers to no one. Yet God brings comfort, tends his flock gently, and provides pardon and strength.

Other passages fill out the picture: God is holy (Isaiah 6:3; Revelation 4:8)—that is, utterly pure and upright and matchless in his manifold perfections. In the triune God there is no moral stain, nor does the Lord author sin or commit acts that are evil (Genesis 18:25; 1 John 1:5; 2 Corinthians 5:21; Hebrews 4:15). Further, God is all-powerful (Ephesians 3:20) and all-wise (Romans 11:33–36).

---

1. John Piper speaks of "regressive sanctification," noting how a believer who fights valiantly against sin and to grow in Christ may later reach a point of "languishing in the wilderness." Progress is not always steady and consistent ("Fighting for Faith with God's Word," http://www.thisisnext.org/resources).

And God is love (1 John 4:8), and his heart of compassion extends toward all (Matthew 9:36; John 3:16; 2 Peter 3:8–9).

The Lord is free and unfettered: "Our God is in the heavens; he does all that he pleases" (Psalm 115:3). His "hand" is not restrained (Numbers 11:23). "Whatever the LORD pleases, he does, in heaven and on earth, in the seas and all deeps" (Psalm 135:6). "Many are the plans in the mind of a man, but it is the purpose of the LORD that will stand" (Proverbs 19:21). "The king's heart is a stream of water in the hand of the LORD; he turns it wherever he will" (Proverbs 21:1).

Isaiah takes up this theme at length: "The LORD of hosts has sworn: 'As I have planned, so shall it be, and as I have purposed, so shall it stand'" (Isaiah 14:24). Similarly, "There is none who can deliver from my hand; I work, and who can turn it back?" (Isaiah 43:13). "I am the LORD, and there is no other, besides me there is no God; I equip you, though you do not know me, that people may know, from the rising of the sun and from the west, that there is none besides me; I am the LORD, and there is no other. I form light and create darkness, I make well-being and create calamity, I am the LORD, who does all these things" (Isaiah 45:5–7). "My counsel shall stand, and I will accomplish all my purpose" (Isaiah 46:10).

God's limitless freedom and sovereignty undergird his work as Creator and Sustainer of all that is: "It is I who by my great power and my outstretched arm have made the earth, with the men and animals that are on the earth, and I give it to whomever it seems right to me" (Jeremiah 27:5). "Ah, Lord GOD! It is you who have made the heavens and the earth by your great power and by your outstretched arm! Nothing is too hard for you" (Jeremiah 32:17). "He [i.e., "the Most High"] does according to his will among the host of heaven and among the inhabitants of the earth; and none can stay his hand or say to him, 'What have you done?'" (Daniel 4:35). "For nothing will be impossible with God" (Luke 1:37).

And so, major strands of the Bible's teaching present God as great and gracious, powerful and kind, wise and purposeful, and beyond reproach in his holiness. This God, the one true Lord of all things, acts with freedom and always accomplishes his purposes. From creation to the outworking of his redemptive designs to the unfolding of his present and future reign, and on to the ultimate, final consummation of his royal dominion, *God is free* and able to do all that he intends to do. No one puts God's arm behind his back. As we turn our attention, then, to the struggle with sin, we begin with the solid foundation of divine sovereignty.

Our Struggle against Besetting Sins

A particular concern is the problem of "besetting sins," that is, chronic patterns of God-dishonoring thought or action. It's perplexing that sovereignty makes space for sin's ongoing existence, but it's a further conundrum that specific besetting sins persist in believers' lives.

When sin takes root in the realm of habit, it can be especially difficult to fight back and gain victory. Richard Sibbes notes, "There are some almost invincible infirmities, such as forgetfulness, heaviness of spirit, sudden passions and fears which, though natural, yet are for the most part tainted with sin."[2] Besetting sins are like ruts in a dirt road—it's easy to slip into them and hard to get out.

Such habits often have a personal aspect, as Satan lures a believer toward sin by appealing to unique points of vulnerability. One person may be especially at risk of falling into gossip, for another it may be greed, for another pride, and for yet another lust (the list could go on). In spiritual warfare the Enemy looks for flaws in our armor and strikes in those places. Through Satan's incessant bombardment targeted at

---

2. Ibid. To clarify, in this study I'm not seeking to distinguish between a besetting (i.e., habitual) sin and an "addiction" to a sinful practice. My assumption is that in either case, the authentic believer will need and want the support of the body and of qualified helpers to assist him or her in the quest for holiness.

our weaknesses, habits of sin often become ingrained, leaving believers feeling trapped and defeated. We groan and weep to find ourselves out on the same battlefield again and again, fighting temptation yet often losing in the war effort.

Thomas Brooks observes, "Whatever sin the heart of man is most prone to, that the devil will help him forward. If David be proud of his people, Satan will provoke him to number them, that he may be yet prouder (2 Samuel 24)."[3] The Enemy seizes upon Ahab's vulnerability to flattery, the readiness of Judas to be a betrayer, and Ananias's willingness to lie for advantage. "Satan loves to sail with the wind, and to suit men's temptations to their conditions and inclinations."[4] The apostle Peter was prone to fear, so much so that he denied even knowing Christ in order to save his own skin. And this besetting sin still lingered in his heart years later when he withdrew from table fellowship with Gentiles and acted hypocritically for fear of "the circumcision party" (Galatians 2:11–14).

Sometimes besetting sins form in the lives of believers who, perhaps through excessive optimism or personal insecurity, are prone to deny their susceptibility: "That's not like me; that wouldn't happen to me!" As a result, blind spots develop, and in the darkness of denial, habitual sins only sink their roots more deeply into the soul. Battling besetting sins becomes impossible if we're unwilling to admit they may exist.

In addition, concealing our sins from others who can encourage us and hold us accountable transfers power to the Enemy, resulting in deep strongholds of besetting sin.[5] When pride or fear protects our secret sins from the loving scrutiny we need from other believers, we greatly compound the problem. In fact, secret lusts sap one's confidence

---

3. Thomas Brooks, *Precious Remedies against Satan's Devices* (Puritan Paperbacks; Edinburgh: Banner of Truth, 1968), 16.
4. Ibid.
5. The more secret sins are, the more difficult they are to overcome (cf. Richard Sibbes, *Bruised Reed*, 106, 111).

in God and hinder the exercise of faith and prayer. Consequently, the soul can no longer "look up," and one becomes barren and useless for ministry.[6] A Christian's whole life can be "arrested" and "all but annihilated" by the influence of a secret sin.[7]

Michael Mangis argues that a believer's sin pattern is like a root system in which all tendrils extend from a central source. So it's important to seek out the primary root sin lying at the core. "The central root will be an old familiar nemesis."[8] When we identify and "name" our root sin, "we have taken a greater level of ownership for it. The naming of the signature sin is the most important step in conquering it."[9] Knowing, for example, that fear is the driving force behind one's typical acts of sin helps one get beneath surface manifestations and address primary issues. John Piper, similarly, stresses the advantage of naming the biblical commands one frequently breaks as a way of cutting through the fog of vague guilt feelings. This way you look your sins in the eye, and instead of whining about feeling lousy, you can deal directly with Christ by confessing and seeking help for putting such sins to death.[10]

Before looking more closely at how the Lord operates in relation to besetting sins to achieve his sovereign purposes, it's important to underscore the warning against reckless, persistent rebellion in

---

6. John Owen, *Sin and Temptation*, 86–87 (cf. Ps. 40:12), 174.

7. Alexander MacLaren, "Secret Faults: Exposition of Psalm 19:12," http://www.ccel. org/ccel/maclaren/psalms.ii.viii.html. (Draw near to Christ and you'll discover many of your secret sins.) See further the discussion of James 5:16 ("Confess your sins to one another") in chap. 8.

8. Michael Mangis, *Signature Sins,* 61. Richard Baxter ("Directions for Hating Sin") urges believers, "Bestow your first and chiefest labour to kill sin at the root; to cleanse the heart, which is the fountain; for out of the heart come the evils of life." He goes on to name several "master-roots," such as ignorance, unbelief, inconsiderateness, selfishness, and pride.

9. Mangis, 63.

10. John Piper, "How I Approach God When Feeling Rotten," http://www.desiring-god.org/Blog/1499_How_I_Approach_God_When_Feeling_Rotten. Richard Baxter ("Directions for Hating Sin," http://www.puritansermons.com/) warns believers, "Be acquainted with your bodily temperature, and what sin it most inclines you to."

Hebrews 10:26–27: "For if we go on sinning deliberately after receiving the knowledge of the truth, there no longer remains a sacrifice for sins, but a fearful expectation of judgment, and a fury of fire that will consume the adversaries." This text teaches that there are besetting sins that lead to final ruin.

It would be going too far to infer that all experiences of recurring sin and all ruts of wickedness signify that one is apostate. After all, the words of warning in Hebrews and the admonitions to encourage one another to turn away from sin (3:12–13; 10:23–25) address ongoing sin among believers. Imperfect Christians are not written off as being "too far gone." In fact, the writer of Hebrews asserts, "Yet in your case, beloved, we feel sure of better things—things that belong to salvation" (6:9).

The key to addressing this dilemma is to focus on the heart. While sincere believers do stumble and stray, they're not at peace with such conduct. In fact, they *cannot* indefinitely snub the Lord and ignore his call to the obedience of faith. The conscience is troubled; the heart isn't at peace with ongoing acts of sin. For this reason, the person who's troubled and torn about whether he or she has committed the unpardonable sin is, in all likelihood, not guilty of that offense (cf. Matthew 12:31). Having a humble heart that yearns for God's honor and for progress in holiness suggests the presence of God's Spirit within, regardless of wayward conduct.[11]

Of course, since the heart is the key, it won't always be possible to differentiate between Christian and non-Christian sinners by outward observation. Ultimately, it's the Lord who looks upon the heart and knows his own (1 Samuel 16:7; John 10:27), and it isn't necessary for humans to be able to spell out the precise makeup of the "invisible church" (i.e., all who truly trust in Jesus Christ). When affliction strikes, however, the pious front of religious nonbelievers often col-

---

11. Richard Sibbes states that God's children "never sin with full will" (*Bruised Reed*, 60).

lapses, and the heart's lack of peace with God comes to the surface. A "severe mercy" of this kind, in fact, can open the door to genuine confession of sin and conversion to Christ.

In any case, it's important to underscore the insidious dangers of besetting sins, for even if their presence doesn't prove that one is unsaved, they can still bring tremendous damage to the joy and peace and mission-oriented living the Lord desires for his people.

Sin can be compared to the bloodsucking tick that not only clings to a living creature but also infects it with a devastating sickness. Lyme disease is transmitted by deer ticks, and when those ticks end up on people, there can be debilitating consequences. Sin that takes hold and becomes habitual also brings devastating effects. In light of this, the bold warning in Hebrews 10:26–27 can serve as good preventative medicine for God's people, even if we may feel confident of better things in keeping with salvation.

The Lord Turns Evil to Good

After this foray into the grim dimensions of sin, especially the disturbing reality of Christians' besetting sins, we come back to the question, Why does God transform his people's lives progressively and not instantaneously, thus necessitating their ongoing experience of sin? And why allow sin to have such *deep* inroads into the lives of God's people—into hidden realms and the inner reaches of habit? Looking closely at besetting sins reminds us that it's a weighty and wrenching matter to live with sin's chronic presence. And yet, despite sin's insidious nature, it's important to remember the biblical truth that God orchestrates all things, even sin's lingering existence, toward his ultimately good purposes. In other words, it's not as though the Lord has compromised his moral purity or sovereign power by bringing sanctification about gradually or by allowing his people to face besetting sins.

Romans 8:28 is a pivotal text here: "And we know that for those who love God all things work together for good, for those who are called according to his purpose." In the immediate context, "all things" includes the groanings of the present age in which believers, like creation itself, yearn for the completion of their adoption and redemption in the fullness of the coming age. Under the weight of today's weaknesses, God's praying people are sometimes pressed to the limits of language. But at that point, the Spirit steps in and intercedes on their behalf. In fact, the "all things" in view are precisely the trials of living far-from-perfect lives in a troubled world (besetting sins included) as we await the final "freedom of the glory of the children of God" (8:21). The Lord weaves such adversities into what will be seen as a beautiful tapestry.

Another crucial passage on God's design to turn evil for good is the story of Joseph. Joseph's jealous brothers abused him and sold him as a slave, and he ended up imprisoned in Egypt for years—all undeserved. But God, the key Actor behind the scenes, was "up to something." In time the Lord maneuvered Joseph into an influential office in Egypt in order to save countless lives from a coming seven-year famine. This good end is finally recognized by Joseph, and in Genesis 45:5–9 he says four times it was God who sent him to Egypt. Of course, he remembers how his cruel brothers had shipped him off with traders. But, looking beneath the surface, he sees who was really at work in all those years of pain: *it was God.* The same point is made in Genesis 50:20, where Joseph says to his penitent brothers, "As for you, you meant evil against me, but God meant it for good, to bring it about that many people should be kept alive, as they are today." All the misery Joseph endured was "meant" by God to take place and lead eventually to good ends.

The theme of God's orchestrating all things for good runs through the Scriptures: "But the LORD your God would not listen to Balaam; instead the LORD your God turned the curse into a blessing for you, because the LORD your God loved you" (Deuteronomy 23:5; cf. Nehemiah 13:2). "It is good for me that I was afflicted, that I might learn your statutes" (Psalm 119:71; cf. Isaiah 38:17). "The LORD has made everything for its purpose, even the wicked for the day of trouble" (Proverbs 16:4). "For we do not want you to be ignorant, brothers, of the affliction we experienced in Asia. For we were so utterly burdened beyond our strength that we despaired of life itself. Indeed, we felt that we had received the sentence of death. But that was to make us rely not on ourselves but on God who raises the dead" (2 Corinthians 1:8–9).

So too, Paul's "thorn . . . in the flesh," though it was a "messenger from Satan," served to keep the apostle from becoming conceited. It reminded him of his own weakness and the sufficiency of God's grace (2 Corinthians 12:7–10). In light of the fact that God does "all that [he] pleases" (Psalm 115:3), it becomes clearer now that it pleases him to accomplish his wise and upright purposes through various means including affliction, Satan's maneuverings, and even sin's ravages in the lives of his children—including besetting sins—by turning such evil to good.

Pursuing God's Purposes

But *why* does the Lord operate this way? This is a challenging question because the Bible doesn't address it directly the way it does the fact of God's sovereign overturning of evil for good. And yet, we can draw some careful inferences by looking at related biblical themes. These lead us to the conclusion, ultimately, that the eternal purposes of God can be more readily accomplished by sanctifying his people gradually. Thus, by allowing indwelling sin to linger within them until the last day and by permitting Satan and his demons to do their insidious work throughout this age, God's purposes are better accomplished by gradual sanctification than they could be by instantaneous sanctification. This claim requires unpacking, and in the course of doing so it will be helpful to describe the purposes of God that are advanced through his long-term, progressive design for our spiritual formation.

In a letter to a Reverend Thomas Gillespie, Jonathan Edwards takes up the question of Romans 8:28 and the backsliding Christian. Just *how* does God work for good in such a case? He clarifies that sin is not good in itself, nor does the text suggest that the good that comes to the sinful believer is the best of all possible outcomes—there are degrees of happiness.[12] Romans 8:28 offers no excuse for justifying or tolerating sin. Nevertheless, it is true "that the sin, in general, of Christians, is for their good, in this respect, *viz.* that through the sovereign grace and infinite wisdom of God, the fact that they have been sinful fallen creatures, and not from the beginning perfectly innocent and holy as the elect angels, will issue in a high advancement of their eternal happiness; and that they shall obtain some additional good, on occasion of all the sin of which they have been the subjects, or have committed, beyond what they would have had if they never had been fallen creatures."[13] Edwards adds regarding the stumbling believer: "It may be so ordered, that their being overcome by that temptation, shall be the occasion of their having greater strength, and on the whole, obtaining more and greater victories, than if they had not fallen in that instance."[14]

When we bring together the various relevant claims of Scripture, the implication Edwards puts forward is affirmed—in the eternal scheme of things, a design for salvation that includes a gradual rather than sudden sanctification is for the best. John Owen clarifies that evil isn't given absolutely free rein. God in his providence obstructs and limits sin: "He sovereignly controls sin's eruptions in the world."[15]

---

12. Jonathan Edwards, "Memoirs of Jonathan Edwards: Reply to the Rev. Thomas Gillespie" in *The Works of Jonathan Edwards*, Vol. 1 (Edinburgh: Banner of Truth, 1974) lxxxix.
13. Ibid., xc.
14. Ibid.
15. John Owen, *Sin and Temptation*, 74.

Thomas Watson's book *All Things for Good* is an extended exposition of Romans 8:28. Even temptation works for good—as a tree shaken by the wind is more settled and rooted, "so the blowing of a temptation does but settle a Christian the more in grace."[16] Watson names several ways temptations are overruled for good. Temptation to sin:

- sends the soul to prayer;
- abates the swelling of pride;
- is a touchstone to try what is in the heart;
- fits believers to comfort others in the same distress;
- stirs up paternal compassion in God toward those who are tempted; and
- makes the saints long for heaven.[17]

Watson, however, cautions against distorting the message of Romans 8:28: "But let none ABUSE this doctrine. I do not say that sin works for good to an impenitent person. No, it works for his damnation, but it works for good to them that love God."[18]

In keeping with Romans 8:28, various good ends follow because God allows ongoing trials from sin and Satan until the end of the age. Again, Owen speaks of divine intentions: "Thus God allows one sin to perplex us and gain strength over us, in order to chasten us and allow us to see lukewarmness before the Lord."[19] John Calvin speaks similarly of our ongoing imperfection: "This means, therefore, that we are kept humble and constantly aware of our need to call upon God."[20] In a roundabout way, then, indwelling sin drives believers to

---

16. Thomas Watson, *All Things for Good* (Puritan Paperbacks; Edinburgh: Banner of Truth, 1986), 34.
17. Ibid., 34–37.
18. Ibid., 51, emphasis original.
19. John Owen, *Sin and Temptation*, 166.
20. R. S. Wallace, *Calvin's Doctrine of the Christian Life* (Edinburgh: Oliver and Boyd, 1959), 323. See also Adrian Van Kaam, *Spirituality and the Gentle Life* (Pittsburgh: Epiphany, 1994), 122—repeated awareness of my human weakness keeps me humble.

their knees and puts their focus on the Lord as the source of mercy and life and all things. This magnifies the honor of God and serves the best interests of his people.

Puritan pastor Thomas Brooks points to specific instances of God's allowing "his choicest ones frequently to relapse into infirmities" to keep them humble: "Peter, you know, relapsed often, and so did Jonah; and this comes to pass that they may see their own inability to stand, to resist or overcome any temptation or corruptions (Jude 14, 15, 16); and that they may be taken off from all false confidences, and rest wholly upon God, and always upon God."[21] Norm Wakefield similarly contends that one reason the Lord doesn't remove sin from our flesh when we come to Christ is that its presence motivates us to call on his resources to combat the internal enemy; we mature by coping with the Enemy through our Lord's strength.[22]

In his book *Respectable Sins,* Jerry Bridges also points to God's sovereign good intentions regarding his people's indwelling sin. "It is quite possible that though He is grieved by our sin (see Ephesians 4:30), He may even use that sin to humble us and to exercise us to cry out to Him with a sense of greater dependency. . . . The Holy Spirit will use these times of disobedience and defeat to help you see how deeply rooted your subtle sins are and how totally dependent you are on His power to help you."[23]

It may be shocking that God would operate in such a manner, but Bridges reminds us that some of God's ways are beyond us: "Whatever your circumstances, and however difficult they may be, the truth is that they are ordained by God for you as part of His overall plan for

---

21. Thomas Brooks, *Precious Remedies against Satan's Devices,* 173–74.

22. Norm Wakefield, *Who Gives a R.I.P. about Sin?* (Downers Grove, IL: InterVarsity Press, 2002), 101. Cf. Leanne Payne, *Restoring the Christian Soul through Healing Prayer* (Wheaton: Crossway, 1991), 20: It's necessary "that temptation and trial compel us to face honestly what is in our hearts."

23. Jerry Bridges, *Respectable Sins: Confronting the Sins We Tolerate* (Colorado Springs: NavPress, 2007), 43, 51.

your life. God does nothing, or allows nothing, without a purpose. And His purposes, however mysterious and inscrutable they may be to us, are always for His glory and our ultimate good."[24]

John Piper's recent work *Spectacular Sins and Their Global Purpose in the Glory of Christ* speaks directly to many of the issues before us. His major claim is that everything God allows is permitted purposefully. This is so because God is and always has been able to effect changes in the events of history and because God knows and has always known the future. "What we do know is that God is sovereign over Satan, and therefore Satan's will does not move without God's permission. And therefore every move of Satan is part of God's overall purpose and plan. And this is true in such a way that God never sins. God is infinitely holy, and God is infinitely mighty. Satan is evil, and Satan is under the all-governing wisdom of God."[25] He goes on to say that God created Satan and his followers "knowing what they would do, and that knowledge was taken into account in God's decision to create them. Therefore, the evil that they do in the world is part of how the greatest purpose of God will be accomplished."[26]

Spectacular Sins addresses the question of how far God's sovereign hand reaches into the tumultuous realities of human history, and the answer is a bold exclamation point behind the "all things" of Romans 8:28 (even though Romans 8:28 isn't cited). "The aim of this book has been to show that over and over in the history of the world, the epoch-making sins that changed the course of history never nullified but only fulfilled the global purposes of God to glorify his Son and save his people."[27] The focus of the book is on the way God has worked in and around certain specific sinful acts, however, so the work doesn't directly address the phenomenon of chronic, indwelling sin as part of

---

24. Ibid., 74.
25. John Piper, *Spectacular Sins,* 47–48.
26. Ibid., 48–49; cf. 54, 56, 58, 69, 103. An obvious implication is that the cross was not "Plan B," but a part of the wise and good design of God from all eternity (58).
27. Ibid., 97.

the lifelong atmosphere of every Christian's life. It's clearly implied, however, that even indwelling sin and besetting sins are among the evils God turns for good by his sovereign hand.

Indwelling Sin as Medicine

Richard Sibbes, a seventeenth-century pastor and theologian, argues that, under the sovereignty of God, sin becomes a kind of medicine: "Diseases are suffered, to put us in mind of infirmities in the root, which we knew not before. For if these should not sometimes break forth into a disease, we would think our nature were pure."[28] Thus the sins of David, Peter, and other believers in the Bible show that it's useful at times to have our corruptions break out and remind us of our weakness and the depth of our perversion and thus help us learn to stand stronger in the future. Sibbes goes on: "It is not sin that damns men, but sin with the ill qualities, sin unconfessed, not grieved for, and unresisted, else God hath holy ends in leaving corruption in us, to exercise, try us, and keep us from other sins. Therefore sin is left uncured."[29]

In an ironic sense, then, sin is left uncured so that it can be part of the cure for sin in the life of the believer: "Where the work of grace is begun, sin loses strength by every new fall; for hence issues deeper humility, stronger hatred, fresh indignation against ourselves, more experience of the deceitfulness of our hearts, renewed resolutions until sin be brought under. That should not drive us from God, which God would have us make use of to fly the rather to him."[30]

---

28. Richard Sibbes, "The Returning Backslider," in *The Complete Works of Richard Sibbes*, vol. 2 (Edinburgh: James Nichol, 1863), 314; cf. Jeremy Taylor, *Holy Living* (London: Henry G. Bohn, 1858; Orleans, MA: Paraclete, 1988), 96: every unpleasant accident, though it taste bitter, "is intended for health and medicine."
29. Richard Sibbes, "The Returning Backslider," 314.
30. Richard Sibbes, "The Soul's Conflict with Itself, and Victory over Itself by Faith," in *The Complete Works of Richard Sibbes*, vol. 1 (Edinburgh: James Nichol, 1863), 231.

In *The Bruised Reed,* Sibbes argues further, "When he [i.e., a Christian] is conquered by some sins, he gets victory over others more dangerous, such as spiritual pride and security. . . . Weakness with watchfulness will stand, when strength with too much confidence fails. Weakness, with acknowledgement of it, is the fittest seat and subject for God to perfect his strength in; for consciousness of our infirmities drives us out of ourselves to him in whom our strength lies."[31] And so, the existence of indwelling sin has the twin positive functions of humbling the heart and directing one's trust toward Christ. "Hence also it is that we are stronger after defeats, because hidden corruption, undiscerned before, is now discovered, and thence we are brought to make use of mercy pardoning and power supporting."[32]

As medicines go, we may say that experiencing lifelong progressive sanctification, along with its flipside of ongoing indwelling sin, leaves a sour taste. But in terms of physical or spiritual medicine, the crucial matter has to do with the patient's overall health: Does a bitter pill lead to genuine wellness in the end? If some medicine or even invasive surgery is necessary to fight off a deadly disease, the course of action is good. B. B. Warfield concedes that submitting to this lifelong health regimen is a "weary process" for the believer. "But it is God's way. And He does all things well."[33]

With a View toward Heaven

Getting a proper perspective on the reality of indwelling sin under the umbrella of divine sovereignty requires an eye toward eternity. Even though God works all things—besetting sins included—for our good, we don't recognize all the benefits of his designs right now. We've spent time asking *why* of God's ways, but not much about *when*: when does

31. Richard Sibbes, *Bruised Reed,* 95–96.
32. Ibid., 116.
33. B. B. Warfield, *Perfectionism,* Samuel G. Craig, ed. (New York: Oxford University Press, 1958), 464.

God finally complete all that's involved in accomplishing his sovereign good purposes through our indwelling sin?

The *when* question is crucial since God doesn't experience time the same way we do—his designs reach far beyond our brief earthly life spans. Further, the Lord has all eternity in which to unfold his infinitely exquisite purposes and ingenious strategies. The patriarch Joseph lived to understand *why* he endured such trials, that his brothers had meant to harm him, but that their acts had put Joseph in a path that eventually led to the protecting of many lives (Genesis 50:20). The positive outcome became evident.

But not all believers have it that way. Many sincere Christ-followers face great trials and live to understand little or nothing of *why*—of how it all works out ultimately for good. Certainly the martyrs in Scripture (e.g., Acts 7:60; 12:2; Hebrews 11:35–38; Revelation 6:9) did not themselves see how their suffering led to good ends in this world (though, to be sure, the effect of such martyrdom on others was often spiritually profound). Contemporary examples of wretched abuse and horrible suffering due to sin may seem to defy explanation. How can such evil ever be turned toward good ends? At times we can't find an answer. No doubt some of God's mysterious designs will come clear only in the light of his glorious face in the world to come.

Having an eye toward heaven will also help me avoid giving the impression that the thoughtful reader should find full intellectual and emotional satisfaction through the case made in these pages. Frankly, I'm convinced that the unfolding and expounding of some facets— major aspects—of the divine plan await the age to come. And, of course, the Lord is free to work out his elegant cosmic purposes over time. Further, our minds are very limited in this earthbound existence, and our emotions are shifting and unsteady. It seems we're not equipped at present fully to grasp the ways of God, including his ingenious plot to turn evil (including our ongoing sin) for good.

As we look in the mirror and see the ravages of sin, and as we consider the pain sin has brought into the lives of loved ones, we yearn for resolution. But are we willing to wait? Can we leave it in God's hands to disclose just "enough" of his sovereign design today and yet to retain vast fields of the splendor of his plan for our enjoyment in the age to come?

I'm not calling for blind faith, and I'm not suggesting we look at today's pain and call it joy. The plundering of human life by Satan's operations and our own sinful ways is grievous, and we do well to weep with those who weep. But in anticipation of the glory of total sanctification in the age to come, we can also rejoice in hope with our brothers and sisters. And further, I think the Scriptures provide more than enough teaching on God's turning evil for good and accomplishing stunning redemptive victories even in the midst of this broken age to give us hope amid the storms—an underlying peace even when all is dark and God seems silent. There's a sound basis for trust in Christ amid our besetting battles and tearful confessions, and a solid footing for hope that the fullness of victory will be ours in his good time.

Until then, we can rest in God's loving care and be assured that he's weaving even our most intense trials and besetting sins together in a beautiful fabric of his sovereign invention. This isn't to "wink" at sin or sweep it under the rug—"Well, my sinful ways are all in God's plan, so there's no problem." Far from it. The heart that's complacent in sin and has a passion for worldly gain but not for holiness is the heart of an unbeliever.

To deliberately go ahead in the ways of sin is to follow the path to judgment and God's wrath (Hebrews 10:26). We're justified by faith alone (Galatians 2:16), but true faith inspires obedience to God (James 2:14–26; Galatians 5:6)—imperfect deeds, to be sure, but real-life change and a genuine desire for Christlike holiness are inherent in the experience of authentic Christian faith (Hebrews 12:14). Romans

6:1 still stands: may it never be that we would let grace become an excuse for sin.

But having said that, the core fact of this chapter stands: the Lord, in his sovereign ingenuity, is maneuvering all things, our indwelling sin included, according to his glorious eternal plan. His saving intentions, set in motion "before the foundation of the world," include the redemption and adoption of a people through Jesus Christ—a plan involving salvation from sin through Christ's death (Ephesians 1:3–14). So the existence of sin was part of the original conception. But this scheme, providing an infinitely valuable inheritance to bless God's adopted children, was always targeted, ultimately, toward the grand end of magnifying the glory of the Lord "to the praise of his glorious grace," as Paul says three times in the first chapter of his letter to the Ephesians.

God's people will be better equipped to praise his glory, even now and especially in the life to come, as a result of being sinners and fighting against besetting sins today, than they would have been if sin had never entered the picture, or if their capacity to sin had been instantly extinguished at the moment of justification. Not only the amazing grace of God to save humans in the first place, but also the amazing *ongoing* grace of the Lord to continue to love and work for good in the lives of his very imperfect children, will serve in the future world to stimulate as yet unfathomable impulses of passionate praise that would never come into being without such acts of grace. This is a good plan—in fact, we can be sure our Lord has devised the *best* plan. He does all things well.

Bibliography

Alleine, Joseph. "Motives and Marks of Growth in Grace." Unpublished letter, 1663. http://www.gospeltidings.org.uk/library/16/7/14. htm.

Barnes, M. Craig. *Searching for Home: Spirituality for Restless Souls.* Grand Rapids: Brazos, 2003.

———. *Yearning: Living between How It Is and How It Ought to Be.* Downers Grove, IL: InterVarsity Press, 1992.

Baxter, Richard. "Directions for Hating Sin." http://www.puritansermons. com.

Beasley, Sabrina. "Help! I Married a Sinner." www.familylife.com.

Bridges, Jerry. *The Pursuit of Holiness.* 3rd ed. Colorado Springs: NavPress, 2006.

———. *Respectable Sins: Confronting the Sins We Tolerate.* Colorado Springs: NavPress, 2007.

Brooks, Thomas. *Precious Remedies against Satan's Devices.* Puritan Paperbacks. Edinburgh: Banner of Truth, 1968.

Bunyan, John. *The Pilgrim's Progress.* Springdale, PA: Whitaker House, 1981.

———. *Prayer.* Puritan Paperbacks. Edinburgh: Banner of Truth, 1965.

Burroughs, Jeremiah. *The Rare Jewel of Christian Contentment.* Puritan Paperbacks. Edinburgh: Banner of Truth, 1964.

Caird, G. B. "Perfection and Grace." In *Duty and Delight: Routley Remembered*. Edited by Robin A. Leaver and James H. Litton. 21–33. Carol Stream, IL: Hope Publishing Co., 1985.

Chester, Tim. *You Can Change: God's Transforming Power for Our Sinful Behavior and Negative Emotions*. Wheaton: Crossway, 2010.

Coe, John H. "Musings on the Dark Night of the Soul: Insights from St. John of the Cross on a Developmental Spirituality." *Journal of Psychology and Theology* 28 (2000): 293–307.

———. "Spiritual Theology: Bridging the Sanctification Gap for the Sake of the Church." *Journal of Spiritual Formation and Soul Care* 2.1 (2009): 4–43.

Crabb, Larry. *Inside Out*. Colorado Springs: NavPress, 1988.

———. *The Marriage Builder*. Grand Rapids: Zondervan, 1992.

Demarest, Bruce. *The Cross and Salvation*. Foundations of Evangelical Theology. Wheaton: Crossway, 1997.

Dodson, Jonathan. *Fight Clubs: Gospel-Centered Discipleship*. Austin, TX: Austin City Life eBook, 2009. http://www.austincitylife.org/fightclubs.htm.

Edwards, Jonathan. "Memoirs of Jonathan Edwards: Reply to the Rev. Thomas Gillespie." In *The Works of Jonathan Edwards*, 1: lxxxvii–xci. Edinburgh: Banner of Truth, 1974.

———. "Thoughts on the Revival." In *The Works of Jonathan Edwards*. 1: 365–430. Edinburgh: Banner of Truth, 1974.

Fénelon, François. *Spiritual Progress*. http://www.ccel.org/ccel/fenelon/progress.html.

Ferguson, Sinclair. *Grow in Grace*. Edinburgh: Banner of Truth, 1989.

Foster, Richard J. *Celebration of Discipline: The Path to Spiritual Growth*. 2nd ed. San Francisco: Harper and Row, 1988.

Gibson, Jeffrey B. "Matthew 6:9–13//Luke 11:2–4: An Eschatological Prayer?" *Biblical Theology Bulletin* 31 (2001): 96–105.

Groeschel, Benedict. *Spiritual Passages: The Psychology of Spiritual Development*. New York: Crossroad, 1983.

Grudem, Wayne. *Systematic Theology*. Grand Rapids: Zondervan, 1994.

Guelich, Robert A., and Janet O. Hagberg. *The Critical Journey: Stages in the Life of Faith*. Salem, WI: Sheffield, 1995.

Harvey, Dave. *When Sinners Say "I Do."* Wapwallopen, PA: Shepherd Press, 2007.

Hoekema, Anthony A. *The Christian Looks at Himself.* Grand Rapids: Eerdmans, 1975.

Julian, Ron. *Righteous Sinners: The Believer's Struggle with Faith, Grace, and Works*. Colorado Springs: NavPress, 1998.

Lewis, C. S. *The Problem of Pain*. New York: Macmillan, 1962.

———. *The Screwtape Letters*. New York: Macmillan, 1961.

Lewis, W. H., ed. *Letters of C. S. Lewis*. New York: Harcourt Brace Jovanovich, 1975.

Lovelace, Richard F. *Dynamics of Spiritual Life: An Evangelical Theology of Renewal*. Downers Grove, IL: InterVarsity Press, 1979.

Lundgaard, Kris. *The Enemy Within*. Philipsburg, NJ: P&R, 1998.

MacLaren, Alexander. "Secret Faults: Exposition of Psalm 19:12." http://www.ccel.org/ccel/maclaren/psalms.ii.viii.html.

Mangis, Michael. *Signature Sins: Taming Our Wayward Hearts*. Downers Grove, IL: InterVarsity Press, 2008.

Massey, Craig. *The War within You: A Study of the Believer's Two Natures*. Chicago: Moody, 1987.

McCullough, Donald. *The Consolations of Imperfection: Learning to Appreciate Life's Limitations*. Grand Rapids: Brazos, 2004.

McKinley, Michael. "Something for Holy People to Glory In." http://blog.9marks.org/2009/04/something-for-holy-people-to-glory-in.html.

McMinn, Mark R. *Why Sin Matters: The Surprising Relationship between Our Sin and God's Grace*. Wheaton: Tyndale, 2004.

Meyer, F. B. *Christian Living*. New York: Revell, 1892.

Munger, Robert Boyd. *My Heart—Christ's Home*. Downers Grove, IL: InterVarsity Press, 1986.

Murray, Andrew. *Absolute Surrender*. http://www.ccel.org/ccel/murray/surrender.html.

Murray, John. *Redemption Accomplished and Applied.* Grand Rapids: Eerdmans, 1955.

Needham, David. *Birthright: Christian, Do You Know Who You Are?* Revised ed. Sisters, OR: Multnomah, 1999.

Neill, Stephen. *Christian Holiness.* New York: Harper, 1960.

Nelson, Peter K. "Abiding in Christ yet Struggling with Sin: Pursuing Contentment on the Long Road of Spiritual Formation." Seminar Paper, Evangelical Theological Society Annual Meeting, Valley Forge, Pennsylvania, 2005. http://sinandspiritualformation. blogspot.com.

———. "Discipleship Dissonance: Toward a Theology of Imperfection amidst the Pursuit of Holiness." Seminar Paper, Evangelical Theological Society Annual Meeting, San Antonio, Texas, 2004. http://sinandspiritualformation.blogspot.com.

———. "Impractical Christianity." *Christianity Today* (September 2005): 80–82.

Owen, John. *Sin and Temptation: The Challenge to Personal Godliness.* Classics of Faith and Devotion. Edited by James M. Houston. Portland: Multnomah, 1983.

Packer, J. I. *A Quest for Godliness: The Puritan Vision of the Christian Life.* Wheaton: Crossway, 1990.

———. *Faithfulness and Holiness: The Witness of J. C. Ryle.* Wheaton: Crossway, 2002.

———. *Keep in Step with the Spirit.* Old Tappan, NJ: Revell, 1984.

———. "The 'Wretched Man' Revisited: Another Look at Romans 7:14–25." In *Romans and the People of God: Essays in Honor of Gordon D. Fee on the Occasion of His 65th Birthday.* Edited by Sven K. Soderlund and N. T. Wright. 70–81. Grand Rapids: Eerdmans, 1999.

Peterson, David. *Possessed by God: A New Testament Theology of Sanctification and Holiness.* New Studies in Biblical Theology. Grand Rapids: Eerdmans, 1995.

Piper, John. *Desiring God: Meditations of a Christian Hedonist.* 3rd ed. Sisters, OR: Multnomah, 2003.

———. *Finally Alive: What Happens When We Are Born Again.* Ross-shire, Scotland: Christian Focus, 2009.

———. *Let the Nations Be Glad!* 3rd ed. Grand Rapids: Baker, 2010.

———. "Letter to a Friend concerning the So-Called 'Lordship Salvation.'" In *The Pleasures of God.* 279–305. Portland: Multnomah, 1991.

———. *Spectacular Sins and Their Global Purpose in the Glory of Christ.* Wheaton: Crossway, 2008.

———. *This Momentary Marriage.* Wheaton: Crossway, 2009.

Plantinga, Cornelius. *Not the Way It's Supposed to Be: A Breviary of Sin.* Grand Rapids: Eerdmans, 1995.

Ryken, Leland. *Worldly Saints: The Puritans as They Really Were.* Grand Rapids: Zondervan, 1986.

Sande, Ken. *The Peacemaker: A Biblical Guide to Resolving Personal Conflict.* 2nd ed. Grand Rapids: Baker, 2003.

Sanders, J. Oswald. *Spiritual Maturity.* Chicago: Moody Bible Institute, 1962.

Scazzero, Peter. *Emotionally Healthy Spirituality.* Nashville: Integrity, 2006.

Scazzero, Peter, with Warren Bird. *The Emotionally Healthy Church: A Strategy for Discipleship That Actually Changes Lives.* Grand Rapids: Zondervan, 2003.

Sibbes, Richard. "The Art of Contentment." In *The Complete Works of Richard Sibbes.* 5:177–93. Edinburgh: James Nichol, 1863.

———. *The Bruised Reed.* Puritan Paperbacks. Edinburgh: Banner of Truth, 1998.

———. "The Returning Backslider." In *The Complete Works of Richard Sibbes.* 2:249–435. Edinburgh: James Nichol, 1863.

———. "The Soul's Conflict with Itself, and Victory over Itself by Faith," 1:119–294. In *The Complete Works of Richard Sibbes.* 7 vols. Edinburgh: James Nichol, 1863.

Sider, Ronald J. *The Scandal of the Evangelical Conscience.* Grand Rapids: Baker, 2005.

Smart, Dominic. *When We Get It Wrong: Peter, Christ and Our Path through Failure.* Carlisle, UK: Paternoster, 2001.

Stackhouse Jr., John G. "What Scandal? Whose Conscience? Some
    Reflections on Ronald Sider's *Scandal of the Evangelical
    Conscience.*" *Books and Culture* (July–August 2007): 20–21,
    41–42.
Tozer, A. W. *The Pursuit of God.* Harrisburg, PA: Christian Publications,
    1948.
Tripp, Paul David. *Broken-Down House: Living Productively in a World Gone
    Bad.* Wapwallopen, PA: Shepherd Press, 2009.
Van Kaam, Adrian. *Spirituality and the Gentle Life.* Pittsburgh: Epiphany,
    1994.
Wakefield, Norm. *Who Gives a R.I.P. about Sin?* Downers Grove, IL:
    InterVarsity Press, 2002.
Wallace, R. S. *Calvin's Doctrine of the Christian Life.* Edinburgh: Oliver and
    Boyd, 1959.
Warfield, B. B. *Perfectionism.* Edited by Samuel G. Craig. New York:
    Oxford University Press, 1958.
Watson, Thomas. *All Things for Good.* Puritan Paperbacks. Edinburgh:
    Banner of Truth, 1986.
Wesley, John. *A Plain Account of Christian Perfection.* http://www.ccel.org/
    ccel/wesley/perfection/files/perfection.html.
Whitney, Donald S. *Spiritual Disciplines for the Christian Life.* Colorado
    Springs: NavPress, 1991.
Wilhoit, James C. *Spiritual Formation as if the Church Mattered: Growing in
    Christ through Community.* Grand Rapids: Baker, 2008.
Willard, Dallas. *The Divine Conspiracy: Rediscovering Our Hidden Life in
    God.* San Francisco: Harper, 1998.
———. *The Great Omission: Reclaiming Jesus' Essential Teaching on
    Discipleship.* San Francisco: Harper, 2006.
———. *Renovation of the Heart: Putting on the Character of Christ.*
    Colorado Springs: NavPress, 2002.
———. *The Spirit of the Disciplines.* San Francisco: Harper and Row, 1988.
Yaconelli, Michael. *Messy Spirituality: God's Annoying Love for Imperfect
    People.* Grand Rapids: Zondervan, 2001.